212 ✓

This book is to be returned on or before
the last date stamped below.

Why Believe in God?

Michael Goulder and John Hick

SCM PRESS LTD

334 01787 4

First published 1983
by SCM Press Ltd
26–30 Tottenham Road, London N1

Phototypeset by Input Typesetting Ltd
and printed in Great Britain by
Richard Clay (The Chaucer Press) Ltd
Bungay, Suffolk

Contents

Preface

John Bowden

This book grew out of a Day School held in the University of Birmingham on 6 November 1982, and organized by the University's Department of Extramural Studies. During the day, the four central chapters were given as pairs of lectures, in a slightly different order, and each session ended with a lengthy period of questions and discussion, in the light of which the text has subsequently been revised.

For publication, at the beginning of the book Michael Goulder has added a chapter explaining the factors which led him, in 1981, to announce that he had ceased to believe in God and was resigning from the ordained ministry of the Anglican church. As a conclusion, John Hick outlines a number of other issues which would be relevant in a full-scale discussion of the alternative perspectives of theism and atheism, and relates his debate with Michael Goulder to other published writing on the question, not least Don Cupitt's two recent books *Taking Leave of God* and *The World to Come*.

I was Chairman during the Day School, and it proved a memorable experience. Almost two hundred people gave up a whole Saturday to be present, and had paid a fee to do so, which is itself an indication of the drawing power of the subject. Their ages ranged from around twenty to around eighty, and they were clergy, teachers, lecturers, students and just ordinary people. Their contribution to the discussion was a particularly important feature of the day; the questions were always relevant and interesting, and often very penetrating, ranging from learned ones about 'epistemic distance' to deceptively simple ones, like that addressed to John Hick: 'Is God ever surprised?'

The answers to the questions, and the papers which preceded

them, were even more remarkable. Here were two men, one who believed in God and one who did not, who were discussing their beliefs without any of those undesirable characteristics which often mar such confrontations. They were colleagues and long-standing friends, not sparring partners, so that this discussion has the character of a joint exploration, rather than being a duel in which one seeks to score debating points off the other. They had worked alongside each other in the same university over a considerable period and were therefore familiar with each other's thinking, so that the exchanges in the debate keep firmly to the same subject matter; they are very much two different views of basically the same landscape and not, as often seems to be the case, views of quite different scenery. Lastly, anyone reading this book will immediately be aware of the deep personal involvement each man has in the question to which he is responding. During the course of their discussion, both John Hick and Michael Goulder, by speaking of their profoundest experiences and convictions, revealed aspects of themselves and factors in their lives of which I – and presumably the audience – had previously been unaware. In so doing they were responding openly and honestly to the demands made by the discipline of theology if it is really to be taken seriously: it is a quest which claims the whole person, not only in his or her thinking but in the way in which he or she lives out their life.

As John Hick reminded us, there is no neutral ground between the alternative perspectives of theism and atheism; one has to respond personally to the reality that is perceived. So even a Chairman cannot be indifferent. That Saturday will remain with me for a long time; and if my own thinking is closer to John Hick's than to Michael Goulder's, I have to record the considerable sympathy and understanding for Michael Goulder's position which I sensed among the audience. If the churches, too, are to respond to reality in our time, they should notice that before making comments on belief and unbelief.

1 The *Fram* Abandoned

Michael Goulder

'Now,' says King Solomon, 'I was a child of parts, and a good soul fell to my lot.' For the first I might, in my lesser way, say the same, but for the second, I am concerned to stress that the 'soul' that came my way was not so much good as biddable. It has been less biddable in middle life, but in early years it had little option. My father was a man much liked, and kindly; but he was sixteen stone, with a moustache, and brooked no disobedience. He had high and extensive ambitions for me, and directed my every step; and for all his affection for me, and pride in me, I found him on the formidable side. I shall always be grateful to my dear mother, and nanny, who were fond of me, and were less exacting.

Being a child of parts, I found no difficulty in leaping the academic hurdles that were set before me at Wagner's primary school, the best (it was believed) in London; and of course this suggested to my father and other mentors the possibility of my leaping more hurdles. I should go early to preparatory school, I should get a scholarship to Eton, and another to Cambridge, and thence to 'the Diplomatic'. The first three of these I in fact achieved: but when I was sixteen, my father was killed in the war – a tragedy for our close-knit family, even if it was to give me a little more space to breathe, and to be myself. However, to give an instance of my dutiful approach to life, when I was six, my first term at Wagner's, I was introduced to Religious Knowledge with the story of Adam and Eve; after which Miss Bird instructed us to draw a picture. She did not specify, so I drew a picture of pirates, which seemed to me more interesting than the Bible. Imagine my chagrin when I was asked which, out of Smee and Captain Hook, was Adam, and which was Eve! Red-faced, I determined to make up

1

for my error, and the following week, while the others were drawing Noah's Ark, I drew Adam and Eve: and so on through the term – while they drew Abraham, I drew Noah's Ark; while they drew Moses, I drew Joseph, and so on. It was seven weeks before Miss Bird suggested that I might now catch up with the class.

While I was at Wagner's, kind uncles and godfathers often gave me books; and two of these, which I at once loved dearly, were children's poems by Herbert and Eleanor Farjeon, *Kings and Queens* and *Heroes and Heroines*. The verses were lively, and sometimes moving, and they appealed to the idealistic streak in me. The last poem in the second book (not by any means the best) was about the Norwegian explorer, Nansen, and in a way has provided the imagery for my life. Nansen wanted to do a great thing, to sail up into the Arctic, and to reach the North Pole across the ice. He sailed his specially-built ship, the *Fram*, into the ice-pack and set off over the ice; but he never reached the Pole. However, he did not die in the endeavour; he turned south over the ice, and reached land, and was rescued. So although his great ambition did not succeed, it was a great ambition, and he lived to do other fine things. The opening lines of the poem were:

> This is the saga of Nansen, the pioneer of the North,
> The saga of Fridtjof Nansen, and the *Fram* that bore him forth.

and the last ran:

> This is the saga of Nansen, who for the Pole set forth,
> And left the *Fram* abandoned to silence in the North.

During these early years, I was introduced to the pallid mysteries of the Church of England at St Jude's, Courtfield Gardens, where I attended, irregularly and without edification, from admiration of one Mary Stapleton. But it was at Wagner's that I joined the C of E with commitment. There history, the most influential of lessons, was taught (in complete innocence) with an unashamed Anglican prejudice. We sat struck in horror by the dreadful tale of the Marian burnings. With halting voice Mr Lefroy told us of Bishop Latimer's courageous words to his fellow-martyr at the stake: 'Be of good cheer, Master Ridley: we shall this day light such a candle as I trust shall never be put out.' No, I thought; and while I live, that candle shall not be put out. Mr Lefroy did not tell us of the

2

brave deaths of the Roman Catholic martyrs: he had not heard of them. But it was from such experiences that I came to be in a genuine sense a member of the Church of England, which, with all its failings, I have never ceased to love. Perhaps also it is from this source that there wells in me a deep suspicion of Catholicism to this day.

With one exception I pass over my four not very happy years at Highfield, my preparatory school. I was too clever to fit in easily, and through the school's lack of imagination never had contact with boys of my own age until my last year; and then, at thirteen, I was confirmed. We were prepared for the great day by the Headmaster, Bug, as he was known, a canon of the church, pompous, charming, a man of business, paternal, in later years a tyrant. The classes were marked, as I later came to see that confirmation classes nearly always are, with the spurious serious-ness of sudden devotion. It was time for us to be done, and we were doing our best to respond to an artificial challenge. We were warned that when the bishop laid his hands on our heads we should not feel an electric shock; nor did we. I was given a pair of gold cuff-links with the date engraved; and a book, *The Holy Communion*, by W. Walsham How. Bishop How died in 1897.

The Holy Communion marked my first unrewarding steps across the ice-pack; there, for the first time clearly in view, was my Pole Star – I was a confirmed Christian, committed to a lifetime's quest of God. The book was to be used each Sunday morning, at the eight o'clock service – parish eucharists, hymns, breakfasts, were all in the future. On the left-hand pages was printed the Prayer Book service, on the right Bishop How's edifying comments. The opening lines soon became familiar to my retentive memory. 'First of all consider what you are going to do. You are coming to God. God is coming to you. It is not a thought lightly to be dismissed.' I hope that I do not need to tell my reader that indeed I did not dismiss it lightly: nothing could have been further from my obedient character. But although Bishop How succeeded in in-ducing in me a proper sense of awe at the church's central rite, I had to confess that the reality of God's coming to me was very dim. Neither at this period of early devotion, nor in the bright time of my conversion, nor in the halcyon days of my vocation to the ministry, nor (I now recognize) ever, did I have any awareness of God in prayer. This unbroken aridity raises a rather stark dilemma,

3

to which I have now given my uncomfortable answer. Either I have a sort of spiritual tone-deafness, whether innate or from continuing sinfulness; or all the church's saints and devotional writers, and some of my most admired Christian friends, have been deceived, or perhaps are even guilty of something approaching a confidence trick.

Naturally at first I preferred the former option, that the fault lay in me. It was puzzling, because it hardly seemed likely that God would penalize me in a faculty in which lay my ultimate hope of blessedness, the vision of himself. It was suggested to me that the spiritual life was not supposed to be easy, and that this lack of response was a test. Later I was encouraged implausibly to compare myself with St Teresa of Avila, who suffered 'the dark night of the soul' for nineteen years. But the continuing lack of any real consciousness of a divine Being at the other end of the telephone, over a period of forty years, is not to be explained so easily. Nor does the sinfulness alternative carry much more conviction. Of course I could have tried harder, prayed longer, been purer in heart, and so on: but then so could everybody. Further, I have become aware of the sorts of selfishness which make it difficult for people to have relationships on the human plane, and I can easily see that these same failings would frustrate a relationship with God. But then I have had little difficulty in getting on with people throughout my life, and I should have expected to find it much the same with prayer.

I cannot accuse myself of being half-hearted over praying. Between the ages of eighteen and fifty I rarely spent less than half-an-hour each day in prayer: between twenty-three and thirty-nine it was commonly an hour and a half. So much time cannot be spent, even by the dutiful, without some return; and I enjoyed the daily offices, Morning and Evening Prayer, and Compline. The variety and beauty of the psalms, and the endless fascination of the Bible as a whole, were a delight at times and a comfort often. But then the enjoyment was, in part, of an intellectual kind: I found the eucharist and non-liturgical prayer hard work and dreary by comparison, for here it was (very nearly) just me and God, and the heavens were as brass, and there was neither voice nor answer. I took to confession, I went on retreats – indeed, I took retreats, and quite popular ones too. I read many a devotional book. I consulted holy men.

4

Many of the methods of prayer recommended by the latter seemed to boil down to much the same thing. (I am not speaking now of adoration-confession-thanksgiving-supplication, but of the simple matter of making a relation with God; sometimes dignified with the names of meditation, contemplation, affective prayer, etc.). First one read a piece of the Bible, perhaps a story from the Gospels. Then one tried to imagine in as much detail as one could the feelings of those involved, perhaps going by rule through the five senses. Then it was time to make those feelings one's own towards God; and finally there could be resolutions to make these things concrete in the day ahead, possibly selecting a particular text or phrase to remember through the day, a 'spiritual nosegay'. Such exercises I am sure did something to sweeten life, and those humanists are the poorer who allow no space to disciplined aspiration. The fact that prayer turned out, in my view, to be a disappointment (there being no God to communicate with) does not mean that it was a farce, or a waste of time.

The barrenness of the life of prayer did not much trouble me at school, however. Being dutiful, I kept up prayers and communion longer than many of my contemporaries, although encouragement at home was rare; and I was not surprised to hear in due course a remark of the Provost of Eton, an eminent and religious man, Lord Quickswood, referring to 'boring duties like cleaning your teeth and saying your prayers'. Eton religion was only a mild improvement on St Jude's; though the Perpendicular pillars in the College Chapel, and the singing of the psalms to the playing of Dr Ley, were alike majestic.

Eton was not, however, a barren school in other departments of the spirit. It was a marvellous education for me, and mostly a time of great happiness. We were lucky enough to be taught by Richard Martineau, whose gentle influence was a blessing on all whom he taught; and we were lucky enough to be taught the Greek classics by him. He loved these old books, and his enthusiasm was infectious. The most important Greeks he introduced us to were Socrates and Homer. Socrates mattered because he questioned every orthodoxy. He never took the standard view for an answer. I suddenly discovered that there was a radical unclarity about Paul's distinction between soul and spirit, and for that matter mind as well. I shall never be a philosopher, but Richard (as we spoke of him) and Socrates between them taught me that no

5

statement, however sacred, is exempt from the requirements that it should not obfuscate, or be self-contradictory. Richard was himself a pious man, but I soon began to feel that there was an uncomfortable tension between the two authorities the school was setting before us: on the one side the given truths of the Christian Church, and on the other the remorseless questioning of the Socratic method. In the end I came to think that the church is not too interested in the quest for truth – how can it be when it knows the answers already? In particular I came greatly to dislike the tradition of the Roman Catholic Church of never admitting that it had been wrong, but always glossing earlier authoritative statements so as to make them mean something other than their authors intended. Both the Catholics and the biblicists seemed to be involved in semi-continuous dishonesties; and no doubt liberal churchmen have some of the same poison in them, but I never found it so offensive.

But Eton classics were not just Plato: there was Homer, and Aeschylus and Thucydides and many more. Homer believed that life was a tragedy, in which men were the pawns of the gods. Men were (in the last resort) noble, and the gods were, in all resorts, ignoble. The *Iliad* is an incomparable poem, whose thousands of marvellously moving hexameters tell the tragic story of Hector. 'Hector alone defended Troy', and he drove the much stronger Greek armies back to their ships, and he killed Patroclus; and in the end he was deceived by Athena into his fatal contest with Achilles. But they are all tragic heroes: Patroclus who dies, and Achilles who loses his best friend, and Priam who goes through the night to beg his enemy for the body of Hector, his son; and Andromache, Hector's wife, and even Helen, whose adultery brought the disasters upon them all: they are tragic heroines too. Homer said: Life does not have a happy ending; live nobly. And Aeschylus said the same in the *Prometheus* and the *Seven against Thebes*; and Thucydides said the same, telling the history of the Athenian expedition to Syracuse. I was reading these epics against a background of the Second World War, and their message seemed more real than the Divine Comedy of the divinity lessons. Indeed the resurrection ending bore an unhappy resemblance to the *deus ex machina* with which the tragedians contrived an artificial happy ending to their majestic plays.

But the challenge to live nobly was to strike me in a quite

6

unexpected way. I went up to Cambridge (to read more Classics) in January 1946. The place was full of servicemen returned from the war, and we schoolboys were not of much account. Trinity College was large, and I felt lost and lonely after being a minor social success at Eton. After six weeks a nice-looking man, David, called and invited me to come with him to the CICCU (fundamentalist) Sermon on the Sunday evening; I would at that stage cheerfully have gone with him to a nude show or a bullfight, and certainly would not draw the line at a sermon.

The sermon was preached with power, as CICCU sermons were, and I dare say still are. The speaker described the plight of the crew of the submarine *Thetis*, which sank on her trials in the Mersey in 1939, and a few survivors were rescued by fixing a device on to the conning-tower.

They had seventy hours of air, and their only hope of escape from death was by putting their faith in the device that had been fixed to the submarine from above. Nothing that they did could help them; their only hope was in trusting what had been done for them. We have seventy years of air, and surrounding us is the prospect of eternal death. Nothing that we can do can help us to escape; only faith in what God has done for us. . .

The preacher took forty minutes, and he did his task well; on his assumptions, which I shared, his case was unanswerable.

David walked home with me, and invited me back to the standard CICCU cup of cocoa. He wanted my soul for the Lord, and my soul was his for the taking. He was the Gospel fisherman, and I was on his hook, flailing helplessly with my tail, unable to escape. What did I think of the sermon? Well, I thought that it was very good, and had never heard one like it, and could not truthfully maintain otherwise. Would I like a cup of cocoa? Not in the least; the main thing I wanted was to get away from David as soon as possible, but good manners forbade me to carry truthfulness as far as that. So the cocoa was brewed, and the hour of doom drew nigh. Would I like to give myself to the Lord? What could I say? 'But surely I gave myself to him when I was confirmed'? That was sure to draw a saddened smile, for I should then be pretending that I had kept my religion up seriously, which we both knew I had not. 'No, not in the least: I am finding this most embarrassing'? That was sure to draw an even more saddened smile, for I should

7

then be putting my temporary embarrassment before my eternal salvation, and I knew David well enough to know that he would say so. There was nothing for it but to say Yes, and of course that lowered me further into the pit of embarrassment, for the next move was, 'Shall we both kneel down, then?' Totally demoralized, I could do nothing but capitulate. Kneeling! On a carpet! David gave thanks for my conversion, and I rose a saved Christian, born again, dragged kicking and screaming from my womb of comfortable darkness into the strange undesired world of spiritual day.

My astonished reader – particularly any reader who has known me in more recent years – may well be asking himself, 'How can he have been such a simp? Where is Socrates now? Is this what is meant by living nobly?', and similar well-deserved rhetorical questions. I do indeed blush to recall that unhappy scene; but must ask also for a sympathetic reflection on my dilemma. In the world I had grown up in, everyone was a 'Christian'. My family were, the boys at school all got confirmed sooner or later, the masters were: so the existence of God was not in practice to be questioned. I knew of course that there were atheists in the University, but they were Marxists, or profligates, or in some other way undesirable. But none of all these people I had known took their Christianity seriously: that is to say, they did not spend much time in prayer, go to church very often, read their Bibles devotionally, evangelize for the faith. (I might name one or two exceptions to the first three negatives, but none to the fourth.) Now if God is God, then the only way to serve him is wholeheartedly, and anything less than that is hypocrisy. These CICCU people were the first Christian group I had met that seemed to me not to be tarnished with such hypocrisy. David (it had become clear without his pressing the point) got up at 6 a.m. to pray and read the Bible; went to a weekly 'BR' (Bible Reading) and 'PM' (Prayer Meeting); attended College Chapel for form at 8 a.m. on Sundays, St Paul's at 11 a.m. for spiritual nourishment, and Holy Trinity at night to bring others to Christ; and no doubt participated in many other practices too embarrassing to mention. One might feel repelled by it all, but this was the first committed Christianity I had met; and I was quite right not to wish to continue a hypocrite.

Of course mine was not the only option, as I was soon to discover; for naturally it was now my duty to bring my friends to Christ, and that from the following Sunday. How I came to dread those sermons! For I was now the fisherman, and my unhappy (and long-suffering) friends the fish; it was my turn to lay out the invitation, to brew the cocoa, and to carry through the whole red-making ritual. Some of them saw the hook within the worm, and would not take the bait; others came, and wriggled off. But I do not wish that I had declined the CICCU challenge myself, for all that it was to take me half a lifetime and much anguish before I could extricate myself from its results. It was good to look the truth, so far as I could see it, in the eye, and to accept the consequences. It might have been better to do as my friend Robin, the first to resist my clumsy angling: to admire the zeal of the CU, but to hold that it was not according to knowledge. Nowadays I should be cautious about accepting anything into which I was being manipulated, however praiseworthy. But I did not understand the meaning of manipulation then, and it seemed a corollary of holding true and saving belief that one should communicate it to others. It still does.

My converters were nothing if not thorough. I became at once a 6 a.m. riser, a Bible-reader, BR-attender and the rest; and within a fortnight had mortgaged a week of my vacation to go to a conference at Oxford. Two incidents at this conference were to make a deep impression on me. One was before lunch by a fire in Lincoln Hall, when someone made a remark implying that we were descended from Adam. I knew of course that CICCU men accepted the truth of the Bible, but it had not dawned on me that they took it this far. I looked at the man and said, 'You mean you don't believe in evolution?' The words were out before I realized their utter heresy; but to my amazement he looked most shifty, and muttered an inaudible reply. My blood was now up; Socrates would not have disowned me; I went round the group and asked them all for an answer. They were saved by the bell; and a senior and extremely friendly man then came and sat beside me, and asked me to go for a walk with him. As we went past St Cross Church he pulled out a Bible from his pocket, and explained to me how the evolutionary theory could be squared with Genesis 1. I was silent, but unconsenting – I could tell intellectual dishonesty even if I could not tell manipulation, and I was not buying that in the religious parcel.

Not the least manipulative of the performances that week was the final address. The speaker told us of a half-hearted Christian who had been seated in a railway carriage, and the Lord had told him to speak to the man opposite. He had been unwilling, from cowardice, a failing most displeasing to the Lord: but eventually he was driven to obey, the man was converted, and became a famous missionary in Central Africa, saving the souls of thousands. Now I was not the only person among the hundreds present who was going home that day in a railway carriage; and I dare say that many of the others went through the same torments that I did. At first it was easy. The carriage was full, and it was evident that God did not wish me to embarrass all present by broaching the topic of the faith. But then the carriage began to empty, and I began to feel less confident about the embarrassment criterion; after all, the man in the address must have been embarrassed, and his fear of embarrassment had been cowardice. There were now only three people in the compartment, and I reached a slightly dishonest compromise with myself: if we got down to two, that would be God's indication that I should speak. We stopped at Chobham, and a man got out. I grasped at a last straw: if no one got in at the next station and the man remaining did not get out, I would speak. We stopped at Longcross: the longest twenty seconds I can remember. No one came; my man did not move; the train began to pull out. I reached up to my bag for a copy of St John to give me some inspiration as to what on earth to say. Then the man looked up from his book: 'Are you a member of the CU?' he said. I stammered an affirmative. 'Well!' he said, 'I've been a member for twenty years.' I felt like Abraham at the sacrifice of Isaac.

The incident was significant to me for a long period, for it seemed to me that for the first time I was able to discern the action of God. I had always had an uncomfortable feeling when people spoke of having an experience of God, because I had had (as I have said) no awareness of his presence in prayer, and certainly no mini-Damascus-Road moment of visionary splendour. This was clearly a good reason for shame, and a good thing to be quiet about; when I hinted it to David he was plainly disappointed in me. When so many (apparently quite ordinary) Christian people could speak of their experience of God, it was evident that I had no experience because of my lack of obedience; or, not to hedge about, my sin. Perhaps I was not a proper Christian at all; and certainly I could not be wholly with the Lord. But now it dawned on me that perhaps God did not have to be known in naked experience alone. Here, despite my inglorious vacillation, I had at the crisis girded up my loins to action of obedience; and lo, the answer had come from heaven in a coincidence otherwise inexplicable. Once I made the first frail response, there was God at once, swift to my aid. All the jargon about unconditional demand and ultimate succour, which I was later to mop up, could be given meaning from this incident. But more important, here we already have the seeds of the dilemma which was to overshadow my life increasingly, and which is described in this book. The basis of religion which made me so uncomfortable was the 'experience-alone' basis which John Hick advocates in Chapter 2; an experience which I have never had, and which I have not lacked willingness or effort to receive. The basis of religion to which I was turning was the 'red-blooded' theology which is described in Chapters 4 and 5, with the reasons for rejecting it.

My days in CICCU were numbered from the moment of the St Cross walk. I could not stay long in an organization that defied science, biblical criticism and common sense, and which insisted on an evangelistic policy which I found increasingly repulsive as well as practically unrewarding. I kept going throughout the summer, and allowed myself to be nominated College Representative for the next year; and also Officer on one of 'Nash's Camps' in August – a so-called Harvest Camp, but the organizers were interested in the harvest of souls, and little work was done in other fields. I went as I had undertaken, but my mind was already made up. I wrote to David when I got home, and resigned, and felt a great load roll off my back. I owed it to the CU that I had resumed my journey to the Pole Star, and with a dedication unknown before; but I had become confident that the bearing they offered was not true north. I turned with gratitude to the liberal, woolly, friendly, lately despised, 'share-our-darkness' alternative, the Student Christian Movement.

The SCM did two things for me, one of which was to be of temporary, one of permanent importance. Immediately it provided me with a sane, spiritual home, where I could work out what I thought with like-minded lost, aspiring souls. The feebleness of the Movement is testified to by the fact that I made no friends in it, and can remember no incident at all in two years of membership at Cambridge. Our chaplain, the amiable Fr Beaumont, composed with-it hymns and ran the College concerts with much beer-drinking camaraderie. I sometimes suspected that our absence of cutting edge might be cause for anxiety, but belief in God was not suspect: the incarnation and resurrection, creation and providence were all rocks upon which unassailable faith was built.

More lastingly, it was the SCM which took me over the class barrier. Social life at home was restricted to the empty middle-class circles which attended Miss Stainer's dancing class and the consequent parties; school had been for those who could afford a private education. But Trinity had a Mission in Camberwell in South London, and I paid two memorable and utterly enjoyable visits to the parish with the College SCM group, one at the annual parish holiday, one *in situ*. It was a revelation to discover that working-class people were so accepting and friendly; conversation was much easier and more enjoyable than in the stilted circles I had frequented, the piety was more genuine, even the girls seemed prettier. Furthermore, the staff of St George's were a wonder: three bachelor priests and a 'lady worker', all devoted Anglo-Catholics. This was in itself a total surprise, since the High Church movement had never touched my life before. There was a prayer for reunion (with the Roman Catholics! – a project inconceivable to me a few months earlier) on the lady worker's wall. Fr Churchill shared a tent with us at night, and got up at midnight to go back to Chapel and say Evensong, because he had forgotten his Office in the haste of the day. Fr Bishop, the vicar, was clearly a good and wise man of spiritual power (he now has the office as well as the name): he told us in a sermon that he had addressed a mob on a bomb-site, vainly trying to persuade them not to throw bricks at a couple on trial for maltreating their child. To see the spirit of devotion and prayer among the parishioners at Compline was an edification in itself. My own possibility of ordination, which had arisen remotely with the CU, now revived on a much more believable basis. Here were sane men in contact with real life, and transparently doing some good.

I had had enough of Classics after two years, and studied Economics for Part II of the Tripos; it was a sensible move to try to escape from the constrictions of my upbringing, even if it cost me two classes (I got a 2.2). Nor did I wish to be ordained, though I did talk to Mr Vallins, our excellent vicar at home. One should, I felt, live dangerously if not nobly, and with my abilities I might achieve much as a Christian in secular life. I toyed with the Civil Service, but their examination coincided with my long-planned first holiday in Italy. The other option was business, and it seemed more adventurous to go abroad than stay in England; so I found myself leaving London Docks on 9 January 1949 bound for Hong Kong, where I was to serve as a junior with the distinguished trading firm of Jardine, Matheson and Co Ltd.

Jardine's was a disaster. The firm was, and is, run by a small group of Lowland Scottish families, and there was no promotion to the top then, however able one might be. But in any case, no one had time to think of promoting, or even training the juniors. As I sailed, Mao-Tse-Tung's armies overwhelmed the Kuomintang; by summer they were in Shanghai; by autumn on the Hong Kong border. The firm's investments – breweries, cotton mills, property, wharves, docks – were lost without a dollar's compensation; the commercial empire accumulated over a century was annihilated in months. What I learned was little, and not good: to play the stock market and to chat up the secretary. I was soon corrupted by the idleness and emptiness of such a life, but fortunately was aware that this was happening, and was even more fortunate to find a way out of my impasse.

Relief from the uncongenial idleness of the office, and the even more uncongenial life of the mess, came in the surprising form of the cathedral. The dean, a dear and good man, to be my friend for life, made me his guest week by week at large Sunday dinner parties, where I met charming and educated people, English and foreign, Eurasian and Chinese, military and diplomatic, government and commercial: this was indeed a happy change from the yachting, racing and sex-talk of the mess. I was introduced to Bishop Hall, a man of towering saintliness, who at once inspired me and my friend John Erskine-Hill to 'adopt' Chinese Boys' Clubs. I would call there for an hour each week, and had much pleasure from joining in their games, taking them swimming and buying them a jersey each for Christmas. The cathedral services were dignified and enjoyable; one could look forward to Dean Rose's sermons. I met Percy Smith, the lively and attractive vicar of Christ Church, Kowloon Tong. In October Alaric Rose asked me if I would consider leaving Jardine's and coming to work on the cathedral staff, first as reader, then as deacon and finally as priest.

So momentous a proposal came to me naturally, and it seemed entirely natural to accept it. Christianity was true, and it provided the means to holy living and ultimate salvation. I was in a life where I was doing no good, and which was doing no good to me: I was being offered the chance of doing boundless good, and here was God showing me the way in. I did not seriously consider not accepting what seemed both negatively and positively a vocation. 'There's not much money in it, Michael,' said Alaric kindly. ' "As poor, yet making many rich" ', I replied unaffectedly, and he chuckled with pleasure. Jardine's released me without trouble, and I started my new life with a retreat on the splendid mountain-top of Lantao Island in February 1950.

The next two years were to be among the happiest in my life. I went to Morning and Evening Prayer in the cathedral daily; read prescribed theology books through the morning; did odd jobs in the cathedral office in the afternoon; and visited in the evenings. It was a lovely life. I was accepted in homes of every sort, and was often treated kindly. My youth, innocence and devotion were passport enough. The Sunday School grew by bounds under my care, numerous young women feeling the divine call to teach under my leadership! I ran the cathedral Fair, was warden of the Hong Kong Toc H, and did a hundred pastoral jobs. I was just thrown in at the deep end and did all the better for it. Alaric might ring up and say, 'Such-and-such a couple have lost their two-year-old daughter. Would you call, Michael, and take the funeral?' I had no idea what to say in these circumstances, and just as well: the parents did not want my vacuous religious comfort, but just to tell a sympathetic representative of the church of the disaster that had befallen them. The only rule was, always go at once. Alaric was also very loyal to me when I got him into endless trouble with hot-headed articles in the *Review* of which he had rashly made me editor. He was a marvellous vicar.

In the meantime I had read a hundred works of theology, and found myself fascinated. Each week would culminate in an hour with the dean or the bishop, to whom I would read my essay. Alaric's comments were invariably interesting and encouraging; the bishop's inspiring, if sometimes tangential. So when the time came for my ordination I was not badly prepared. I had no doubts.

14

I was tolerably schooled in biblical and doctrinal theology, on an already firm linguistic basis of Greek; and could produce a fair statement of liberal Anglican belief on most topics. The baroque splendours of the Christian theological edifice held me in their spell. In particular, the doctrines of the incarnation and the resurrection seemed transparently true, and I was quite prepared to take the offensive for the atonement as well, and for other positions riddled with contradiction. It did not fret me that I felt the presence of God so little, for I seemed to feel his action in answered prayer and in provident guidance of my ways. The huskies pulled my sled easily over the smooth ice that glittered magically beneath the northern lights: the Pole Star lay clear ahead.

The church is maintained to a considerable measure by the holiness of its saints, and I was bound in by knowing not only many good men, especially clergymen, but also one or two Christians of translucent holiness. The first of these was the bishop, R. O. Hall, one of the great missionary bishops whom the Anglican Church has produced. Devoted to his slum parishioners in Newcastle in the 1920s, he had come to be Bishop of Hong Kong and South China in 1932, and for more than a third of the century there inspired all with whom he came into contact. He never spared himself. He sold the Bishop's House garden in town to build a hospital. Beggars thronged his office, and he would intercede for work for anyone. He was up writing letters often past midnight. His home was a constant scene of warmth and hospitality. His official residence was turned into a dozen flats to help this couple or that. As with his own, so was it with the church's resources. When the Communists reached the border, the diocese had a reserve of $106,000: he sent $100,000 to Canton, and kept $6,000. He was constantly a step ahead of the Hong Kong government in providing for social needs. He put his best clergy into St James' Settlement, or St Christopher's Orphanage. He had an enormous programme of diocesan school-building, far exceeding what might have been expected of the tiny Anglican Church. He introduced a Housing Association and other housing schemes before the disastrous Shek Kip Mei fire compelled the Governor to face public responsibilities in this field. Children's clubs, discharged prisoners, clinics, poverty studies, family welfare, there was no area of need where he was not the moving spirit. He designed his diocese to be the church for others.

15

RO's concern was rooted in his religion, and like everything else about him this was felt as well as thought out. He told us in a sermon: 'I am an apostle, because I have seen the Lord.' He had had a vision of Christ alongside him one morning as he celebrated his eucharist. He ended every interview with prayer, and RO's prayers were not the embarrassing CU formulas I had so come to loathe: they were utterly sincere, natural and straightforward, and they left you feeling between tears and ecstasy. He would often end with reciting Wesley's great hymn, 'O Thou who camest from above, the fire celestial to impart. . .': if ever that fire was imparted, it was to, and through, RO himself. His influence was irresistible, especially his humility. My *Fram* was a ship to be proud of.

I left Hong Kong in May 1952, and in September began a further two years of theology, this time at Trinity College, Oxford, under Alaric's old tutor, Austin Farrer. Few men could have been more fortunate than me, to study under two saints: RO in Hong Kong and Austin in England. However, Austin was close to being a genius as well as a saint. His biblical studies were imaginative to the point of intoxication, and were to be the flame to set alight my life's major work. His philosophical books were profound and, where I could understand them, inspiring. His sermons and his humble devotion were my guide for many a year. But I do not wish to exhaust my reader's patience with tales of the good Christians I have known, but rather to explain how I came to turn back from my quest for the divine Pole.

Oxford theology was not a good preparation for a Christian minister: it gave you a competence up to AD 451, which is about as useful for the job as the education received by the Major-General in *The Pirates of Penzance*. Austin advised me to take the special paper in Hebrew, as 'the church needs Hebraists'; and had I retained my early biddableness I should have acquiesced, and never thought again, and lived happily ever after. But the feeling was too like that when I succumbed to reading more and more classics; and I insisted on taking the philosophy option, which at least introduced me to the debate with the positivists. So I became familiar to some degree with the writings of atheists, Russell and Ayer, Wisdom and Flew, and soon found a quick way of despatching their 'sophistries'.

Austin Farrer is the most subtle of writers, and it is no surprise that there is today a growing industry in interpreting his thought. I attended a conference in 1977 in which Professor Elizabeth Anscombe maintained that his view of the freedom of the will was diametrically opposite to that understood by everyone else in the room. He did not assist clarity by refusing to refer to his opponents by name, or to give any footnotes or references; and his later books consist of a sequence of debates in which all participants argue their position in peerless Austinian paragraphs, and the reader is totally convinced by each in turn. So I cannot presume to say what Austin taught about God, but only what I took from him. The reader may check my interpretation with his last book, *Faith and Speculation* (especially Chapter 4), and with the very different view of Brian Hebblethwaite.[1]

Our relation with God, Austin seemed to say, is like a man's relation with his friend. We become friends in this world by trying each other out; we ask a man to a meal, to a concert, to a holiday, to participate in some serious enterprise. Each step encourages us to feel that we know and like, and can trust, him. So personal relations give us dependable results like our relations with things, and may deserve 'the blessed epithet' of empirical, in so far as the matter allows: only, of course, you can never foretell what your friend will do; you only know that he will do something characteristic. Our relation with God is similar. We know that he commands us to a certain way of life, and as we respond to this command, two things follow: the one a sense of blessedness, like the contentment we enjoy in friendship; and the other a consciousness of further commands. The more we obey, the more demanding (and the more satisfying) will be our obedience. It is in the growth of this relation of friendship with God that our salvation lies.

How, then, can we poor amateurs tell the will of God? We discern it, in prayer and with the aid of scripture. There are written the mighty acts of God; and it is the same God with whom we have to do. If a new Constable is discovered in someone's attic, a lover of Constables may know in a minute that here is the touch of the master, even though he has never been trained in art history and technique; and so may a simple believer discern the will and action of God correctly, without having a degree in theology. God's actions are always indirect. We cannot see his eyes twinkling, as we do our friend's. But we may know that it is his characteristic hand at work, as surely as a British desert general, used to cautious Italian reactions, may say as he watches some daring enemy advance, 'This is Rommel.'

How then does God affect our world? Isaiah says that Assyria was the rod of God's wrath on the back of disobedient Judah. He means that the Assyrian king might have sent his armies in many directions, but God made him feel the force of the arguments for a punitive expedition to Jerusalem. The hearts of kings are in God's rule and governance, and he turneth them as seemeth best to his godly wisdom. Further than this it is not profitable to speculate: we cannot know the mechanism by which God moves the causal joint between his action and ours.

Austin's theology was thus, as I have drawn the lines in this book, red-blooded; and in private he would take this a long way. We as students once asked him whether he had ever done a miracle. He was distressed by the dilemma in which we had placed him, but he finally said that there had been one occasion when he had felt moved to pray confidently over a dying man, and he had recovered. But all these things were in the inscrutable will of God, and the man, who was a tramp, had died three months later in a derelict house. So Austin's God took a hand in the world. We could see its main line of action in the biblical story, and could on occasion divine that his particular purposes lay this way or that. We could not reasonably expect to see more than through a glass darkly; and his inscrutable wisdom must always put our doubts to silence.

Oxford was soon a memory when, in 1954, after a summer term at Westcott House, I set forth with my newly-wed wife for the parishes of St Thomas, Pendleton and St Anne, Brindle Heath, in the city of Salford. Salford was bleak, wind-swept and filthy – fogs such as I have never seen before or since – but the people were welcoming, and we enjoyed it. John McClintock, my vicar, was a member of the old Irish Ascendancy, and treated the parishioners as if they were his tenants in County Sligo; but he could see that I wasn't having that, and we got on. The most unmilitary of men, I was made O/C the Church Lads' Brigade; and amazed myself as well as the lads and officers by running a successful camp in the Derbyshire hills. I ran another successful Sunday School, and the

18

teachers used to come up to our house on Friday nights for a preparation class followed by beans-on-toast. The vicar was run over and killed nine months after I arrived, and my delightful fellow-curate was leaving, so I had eight months in sole charge of the two parishes. I took five services each Sunday, and four weddings many Saturdays; I baptized by the dozen and once took forty-one funerals in a week. Besides all these things, there was the care of both the churches, with their history of suspicion and jealousy. One, when inflammatory words had been said in public, I reduced a contumacious parishioner to apology by the threat of excommunication. I worked like a black, and was appreciated. I was feeling my feet as a pastor, and was happy.

After two years Bishop Greer sent me to a parish of my own, St Christopher's, Withington, in South Manchester. It was again a time of hard work, and had its high moments. We were among the first parishes to go in for Direct Giving, and I ran the campaign myself, without the aid of expert fund-raisers. We took seven hundred of the parishioners in twelve double-decker buses to the Urmston Baths (covered over for the occasion) for a slap-up 8/6d dinner. It was a project my father would have been proud of ('Think big', he would say). The bishop came and spoke briefly; my wife was resplendent in cloth-of-gold; a Welsh tenor, known to a member of the PCC, sang a totally unsuitable aria from *Rigoletto*; and I then delivered the crunch £500 sermon. The church's income had stood at £17 per week, and our men's teams were to call on every family represented and ask them to promise what they wished. I would ring the church bell a month later the number of times that we had pounds a week promised; and when the time came, I rang the bell seventy-one times. It was a great moment: my prestige never stood as high again. I did a second campaign to persuade people to the tougher commitment of attending worship, which was a mild success. But my six years at Withington ran out amid sour and petty feelings. I made some mistakes, but the leading members of the PCC were neither understanding nor kind. I was fortunate to have some good friends in the parish who stood by me, some of them people we still see.

No clergyman can survive the slings and arrows of parish life without adapting the clear, bright faith with which he emerged from his theological college; and I was no exception. The principal casualty of my eight years' warfare in Lancashire was my confidence. This was immediately evident on a pastoral level. I worked unstintingly. I rang the bell for Mattins at 7.30 each morning, and the last visit began at 9.30 at night. But it was not evident that so much work, and prayer, and concern, and (to be straightforward) more clear-headedness and imaginative leadership than most parishes could hope for, were bringing home much bacon. The communicants' register (for what such a criterion might be worth) had been fifty on most Sundays before my arrival. For one delirious Sunday I saw it up to two hundred, but it was back in double figures before I left (and drifted further under my successors). Year by year I watched my thriving confirmation classes, junior and adult, wasting away. When times were good I might present forty candidates to the bishop, to the chagrin and envy of my clerical neighbours: but only thirty of these might survive the year, twenty the second year and ten the third. 'Give us grace to persevere' is a hymn-line written by a parish clergyman under threat for his own faith (Percy Dearmer). An honest and intelligent man sought my counsel on prayer, which I was glad to give; but in a week he was back to say that it hadn't worked, and could I make some other suggestion. I could hardly say to him that it had not worked for me either. This failure of the church to grow, this general absence of religion 'working', gnaws the vitals of a parish minister in a way it does not those of a university teacher of the philosophy of religion.

More subtly and slowly came to notice a loss of theological confidence. Wisdom and Flew had argued, sophistically of course, that religious claims like 'God cares for us' are not genuine assertions, but covert encouragements, like 'Keep your pecker up'. I could not help noticing that when I produced my religious stock-in-trade for the comfort of those in need, they would either be silent and change the subject, or would say, 'Yes, Rector; what I always say is, Look on the bright side.' Furthermore, my red-blooded theology was driven to rather frequent dependence on 'the inscrutable wisdom of God'; for instance, when the plane crashed which carried from Spain the much-idolized Manchester United team, I found myself speaking deprecatingly of the idea that God intervenes in the world. I was alarmed to meet a more extravagant form of myself in the shape of the vicar of Sissinghurst, whose church I visited on holiday with an agnostic friend. 'And where do you come from?' he said. 'Really? From Manchester?

Who would have thought that God would have brought you all the way from Manchester to hear his Word in Sissinghurst today?' This was carrying the doctrine of providence a bit far, I felt; but it was, actually, my doctrine of providence. I was beginning to feel the force of what I later came to think of as Goulder's dilemma.

It was a relief, therefore, when the opportunity came to leave Manchester, in the form of a letter from Hong Kong – in fact a series of letters from my old hero, Bishop Hall. Several years before had come an amazing summons from heaven via RO: he was retiring in 1963 – would I be his successor? For while so long ago he had been my pattern of Christian wisdom and service, it appeared that I had equally been idealized for my zeal and devotion. The truth is that the choice was not large of young men known to him as of ability and fervour; but I did not look on the invitation in so realistic a manner, nor did I consider the possibility that the gift of the see did not lie in his hands. The voice of RO was the voice of God.

Now, as I felt the sands running out in Withington, came a more concrete proposal. Would I come out to Hong Kong and be Principal of the Union Theological College? It had only nine students, but it would grow under my leadership. In the meantime, he was not to retire till 1966; and I could see and be seen. In a burst of humility I consulted Bishop Greer, always a kind if exalted figure, on my suitability: he had stopped worrying about his inadequacies, he told me genially, for those of his clergy were so much more pressing. In any case Hong Kong was a small diocese, and I should do little damage.

So my wife and I and our four small children boarded the boat train at Victoria in August 1962 and set out for my second four years in the Colony. It was not less happy than the first. I became fond of the Chinese students in the College, and we were a compact unit. I taught them both Testaments, pastoralia, philosophy, liturgy, ethics, Marxism and a good deal else; for I was the only full-time staff member, and those who came in to teach occasionally were liable to be discovered reading the students their 1930 college notes. To my great relief, however, there was a part-time assistant, an American, Tad Evans; and to my even greater relief, when I asked him what he would like to teach, he replied, 'Doctrine'. So I had breathing space. My wrestling with the providence question could be continued in private.

But not for long. Within a matter of weeks I was reading reviews of Bishop Robinson's *Honest to God*.[2] It appeared from these that it was a shallow book; the Archbishop of Canterbury had spoken against it publicly; Alasdair MacIntyre concluded that the author was a crypto-atheist. But Tad remarked to me casually that he had just read the best book on theology he had seen in ages: 'Not *Honest to God*?', I said, and it was. So began a period of years in which I, like most other clergy, was asked my opinion of *Honest to God* repeatedly; and it was a question which we could not answer, like the Irish question in *1066 and All That*. Robinson had a trenchant, even an unpleasant style, and he set the questions of theology up in the form of antitheses that were far from clear, like the God Up There and the God Out There; but he was plainly doing his best to be honest, and was succeeding much better than I was. Thus he was publicly confessing to the inadequacies of my red-blooded providential view, which he had once held, and to the barrenness of his old-style devotional life: the very topics which I had long been so keen to screen from public view. But when one came to distil what doctrine of God still remained, it was nebulous. It appeared that 'God' was a term meaning 'our ultimate concern', 'the ground of our being', etc., and for practical purposes (including prayer) it seemed that 'God' was equivalent to 'other people'. So if you said you disagreed with Bishop Robinson, you looked, and felt, stuffy and retrograde; and if you approved of him, you invited the supplementary question, 'But what exactly is the difference between him and an atheist?' Not that I much minded calling Bishop Robinson an atheist; but MacIntyre had argued that Tillich and Bultmann were atheists too, and one would have to draw the line somewhere.

But not only was my doctrine of God thus threatened, but my faith in the resurrection, as a clear instance of supernatural action, had taken a knock. A friend advised me to read William Sargant's *The Battle for the Mind*, and I was introduced into a fascinating world of techniques for securing conversion. A number of cases of conversion were described, to Marxism, Voodoosim, Methodism, etc., and the concomitant features seemed often to be the same: a character of a certain type under the pressure of a sequence of 'inhibitions' – intense cold, questioning, repeated disappointments or humiliations, weariness, danger, etc. But then, it struck me, would not all this apply very well to St Peter? He had been repeatedly humiliated: at the Last Supper, at Gethsemane, in the High Priest's courtyard, by the crucifixion. Would it not be perfectly believable that he then experienced conversion in the form of a vision? We already had suggestions of psychological explanations of Paul's conversion, and hysteria had often been alleged for the mass appearances. Peter had been the rock of belief in the reality of the resurrection, because none of these theories covered him. But now it looked as if there was a plug for one more gap in the God-of-the-gaps; and I had had the dubious satisfaction of finding it.

The Hong Kong years passed quickly. My little College was too small to absorb all my energies, and I undertook many extraneous activities. I gave courses of talks on Radio Hong Kong, clergy retreats, public disputations; ran the Diocesan Diploma in Theology (DDT) and the Ministers' Fraternal. But I also took a delight in engaging in political controversies in the papers and on the radio: for Hong Kong was then governed by a conservative Governor, advised by ten civil servants and ten millionaires. I was not always well-informed or judicious, but was frequently effective and correspondingly unpopular. It was a great life.

It was a great life while it lasted. But it had been evident to me after three weeks that my College was Union only in name; it was Anglican in fact, and the church's limitation to one and a half ordinands a year meant a maximum of five full-time students. This was not a proper unit. I could not teach everything well, and the students needed a broader community. I therefore suggested to the bishop that we unite with the two other Protestant Colleges, and spent a good deal of time over the four years making good relations with them. But the Church of England had done its work too soundly. The Chinese canons voted 'not to water down our Anglican standards' in April 1966, and I resigned. The College collapsed under my successor, and the union has now been satisfactorily effected. In the meantime RO had announced his own resignation, and the nominating committee, with commendable vision, invited the eminent Bishop Joost de Blank, once of Capetown, now of Stepney, and he accepted. We left the day after the election. But it was not to be, for de Blank had a heart attack and never came. Not that I should have been elected in any case, for my political activities had made me a source of suspicion and dislike among the English community. And, in view of what was to come, this was just as well.

My friend Joyce Bennett, one of the first three women priests in the Anglican Communion, had seen an advertisement for the post of Staff Tutor in Thelogy in the Department of Extramural Studies in the University of Birmingham. She had thrown the journal away, but it was recovered from the *lap-sap* and the closing date was found to have passed. With nothing to lose I wrote my own reference, and made it sound impressive: 'I read French, German, Italian, Greek and Latin, and speak Chinese. . .' To my surprise I had a letter back offering me a special late interview. That was good news: no committee meets twice unless the field is weak, and within a week of landing I was employed.

But I faced a baptism of fire. I joined my new colleagues for coffee the first morning and sat with two of them. 'My daughter asked me the other day,' said one, ' "Why do people believe in God?" ' 'I suppose,' said the other, 'you told her it was a non-question?' And so on. What should I do? Try out St Thomas' Second Proof on the philosopher? But the daughter's question was an entirely reasonable one, and it shamed me that I could venture no answer to it. I determined to sound out my colleagues in the Theology Department, and arm myself for the future.

I had secured the job by virtue of my writings on the New Testament, and my experience as an adult educator aboard. I was in a position therefore to teach New Testament courses in various centres for a year or two, and to read around and talk to others until I felt enough confidence to launch a defence of the faith. I talked to most of the Theology Department, and was surprised to find that many of them seemed to be as much in the quag as I was. Others could give impressive-sounding accounts of why they believed, but I did not understand them, and the days of my biddable humility were nearly over. I had begun to feel the force of Wittgenstein's dictum: what can be said can be said clearly. Into this unhappy vacuum, a year after me, came John Hick, and whatever failings his critics might accuse him of, unclarity was not one of them. I read his books with enjoyment; heard him read papers with admiration; and found to my delight that he could see force in my own thinking. He asked me to join the Open End

Group, a monthly gathering to discuss the philosophy of religion. The group included the charming but embattled Harry Stopes-Roe, a humanist from my own Department. It was in this company that the battle for my mind was to be waged over the next decade.

But immediately my thoughts moved back into an earlier ambit. I had begun to produce some radical ideas about the Gospels, and Austin Farrer secured me an invitation to read a paper to the Oxford Society of Historical Theology (the dons' biblical and doctrinal group). I wrote on the parables, one of the best pieces I have ever done, and it was received handsomely. This was to lead on to remarkable consequences of both a professional and a religious kind. There is at Oxford a prestigious visiting lectureship, the Speaker's Lectureship, six to eight lectures a year for three to five years; and Austin happened in 1968 to be the Chairman of the Electors. He wrote encouragingly to me to put in an application: 'You will not get it, but it will give me a chance to praise your name in the seats of the mighty.' I had a month to write my prospectus, and determined to see that there were no errors in it; after three weeks came a card, 'Be sure to put in: the field is not large.' In the event there were three candidates: two famous scholars and me. The Electors were to meet in March, but a quorum was not available, and the meeting was postponed till May; and even then only five attended, one of whom was Austin. In the meantime my parables article was published in the April edition of *The Journal of Theological Studies*. Austin wrote me a lyrical letter to tell me that I had been given the Lectureship. This turned out to be the foundation of much work I was later to do; but it is the theological side of the incident with which I am now concerned.

Austin knew that he had had important new ideas about the New Testament, and he was persuaded that some of them were true; but he had not had many pupils who had become New Testament scholars. There was Professor Aileen Guilding at Sheffield, but she was ill and about to retire; and there was me, starting a doubtful academic career at Birmingham at the age of thirty-nine. So the Speaker's Election assumed a religious significance. He ended his letter: 'I think, over this business, divine providence deserves a good deal of credit; for getting your article out in the nick of time, sending various Electors abroad, putting me in the chair of the meeting, and moving the unpredictable heart of the Professor of —.' Austin did not make jokes about God, and his

25

quizzical humour here did not mean that he was not serious. He felt that he could trace the divine hand behind the plans and politics of the academic world, weaving the pattern of his will, as a master oriental carpet-maker works into his design the errors of his apprentices. It was a shock and a great sadness that he died on 29 December 1968, just three weeks before the first of the Lectures so marvellously commissioned.

So for five years I was to make my way to Oxford, and argue my radical solution to the riddle of St Matthew and St Luke; but in the meantime I felt a new confidence in my traditional providentialism, based in part upon so evident an experience, and in part on a constant reading of Austin's philosophical writings. I accepted Harry Stopes-Roe's proposal – and it was nearly a challenge – that we should conduct a 'dialogue-course' together. This meant a series of ten two-hour debates before some fifteen to twenty people, first in Shrewsbury and then in Worcester; and there is nothing like two series of ten two-hour public debates with Harry Stopes-Roe for revealing to a man what his theology is worth. I felt the first series was a drawn battle, with the advantage at times with me. But somewhere on the M5 between Birmingham and Worcester – for the fight went on in the car as well – I seemed to feel a wound in the heart that told me that Austin's doctrine of providence would not do. John Hick was to add the coup de grace by pointing out the arbitrariness of such a God; and John Lucas, by pointing out his manipulativeness.

But if Austin's theology no longer persuaded me, was there not John Hick's? There was indeed, and I began to make this not only the foundation of my own belief, but also of courses in 'Belief in God Today', 'The Action of God', etc., taught in different centres round the West Midlands year by year. These were lively courses, for they were fuelled not just with reading, but with hearing the issues disputed in the Open End Group; and I was drawn into *The Myth of God Incarnate* symposium, so that I was contributing new ideas as well as receiving them. I could often see the force of Harry's objections to John, and took to adopting a sceptical viewpoint in the discussion. 'Your function,' said John Hull, 'is to point out that we are all wearing the Emperor's clothes.'

This newfound scepticism, or at least doubt, was an uneasy companion. At one level it was all right. I had dispensed with providence, with the resurrection and now with the incarnation;

26

intellectually, therefore, dispensing with God was only one step further down the same road. But even academics are men of flesh and blood, and I hope that I have conveyed to the reader something of my attachment to the church: it was no easier for me to renounce my quest than for Nansen to turn south. It was indeed unthinkable; but reality compels the unthinkable to be thought. Worship in church became the driest of duties. The readings were myths; the prayers were no prayers to me; the sermons said nothing, even when I respected the preachers. I felt myself increasingly unable to accept invitations to preach. I found myself bored and exasperated by the obscurities of professional theologians. Others might praise the marvels of Barth and Brunner, Moltmann and Pannenberg, Küng and Schillebeeckx; to me they were repetitious, and often idle rhetoric. But worse was the discomfort of the teaching. My courses on God were extremely popular. Often thirty and even forty people would crowd the room, clergy and lay people alike; in Lichfield, Leamington, Kingswinford, Wolverhampton, Hereford and Birmingham. Controlling the discussion was an art, for the feelings of many of the students were strong. I had the powerful impression that most of them had never heard a fair open discussion of the fundamentals of the faith before, and for all that this was not my speciality, they were getting more out of it than they had from their professors at university or theological college, or their vicars in church. But I could not deceive myself that I was defending the faith, or confirming them in it. I was pushing them from corner to corner, as a cat does a mouse. Here is the red-blooded theology we were taught in the Bible, I would say: that is no good, they would reply. Here is the driven-snow alternative, I would continue; but they did not like that either. I was educating them, and that is what I am paid to do. Good teaching often has an edge of menace, and my courses never lacked that. I taught them as cliff-hangers from week to week, and they kept coming: but I could not help asking questions about my integrity on the way home.

The crisis came with an invitation back to my old diocese of Hong Kong in the summer of 1981. I was asked to deliver the Martin Lectures, the first to be given in honour of a dear good friend, Canon Ernest Martin. I suggested speaking about St Paul and St Luke, but the organizer preferred a more theological topic, so I said it should be on God. But I had not quite allowed for the

27

setting. I was asked to speak in full canonical robes in the Chapel of St John's College to some sixty people, including my old pupils, now vicars of important churches; so the lectures were more like sermons. Furthermore, I took a course for the ordinands, eighteen in number. They had never met so radical a teacher before, nor one who taught by discussion instead of lecturing. I began to feel increasingly the responsibility I carried for seeming to encourage young people to give up promising secular careers in order to enter a ministry in which I could not claim to believe. After the last lecture there was a discussion, and an old friend of mine, Philip Shen, a lecturer in the Chinese University, spoke. 'The critique has been very sharp,' he said, 'but the defence has been rather weak. How far is it possible from such a basis to go on speaking for the church?' The question was a genuine question, not a criticism; but it deserved a genuine answer, and this I now determined to give. My resolve was strengthened by a conversation with a Lutheran scholar at a conference three weeks later. 'I still take funerals sometimes,' he said, 'but it is difficult when you don't believe in the after-life.'

So, sick at heart, I turned my huskies southward. My Pole had been a will o' the wisp. My *Fram*, my beloved church, was locked for ever in the ice-floes of theological contradiction, a barren and chilling waste. My thirty years of high endeavour had been an error. Nevertheless, I think that no endeavour that engages the best one has to give is wasted. I do not repent of my quest. I have brought home much rich experience from my journey, and helped others on the way. I wrote to the Bishop of Birmingham on St Matthew's Day 1981, to resign my orders; and in fact to leave the church.

But was so extreme a move required? My fried Don Cupitt (a far cleverer man than me) had faced my difficulty, and had decided that his place was within the church; and I found that a number of my close friends had been moving in the same direction but felt that they could still call themselves Christians. After all, Don argues, religion does not consist only of a set of beliefs (though that is where the semitic religions, Judaism, Christianity and Islam have laid the stress). There is the religion's story, or myth; its liturgy and ritual; its ethical system; its social pattern; and so on. Sometimes, as in India, these aspects – or, as Ninian Smart has called them, dimensions – of religion may be much more important than the belief system, which in any case is never monolithic. For us today the old Christian belief system, with its objective God, is not a valid option. But why should we not dispense with this metaphysical superstructure and retain the rest? Mainstream Buddhism has no belief in God, but a discipline of meditation and a way of holy life; and these are things which Christianity also provides. People need a story for inspiration, and a liturgy to express life's mystery, and an ethic to live by; religion is important to them. But despite the lapse of belief, the church, at a different level, remains very strong. People use religious language still, but not so much to assert claims about another world as to give force to their ethical convictions; as when the 1980 earthquake in Southern Italy was felt as a call to practical religion rather than a problem in speculative theology. We cannot leave the church: that would be to slide into a cultural crisis in which the only moral judges are force and fashion. Rather, we should purge the church of its supernatural beliefs and nurture its spirituality and way of life.[3] The world needs the church, and the church needs its radicals, who alone will face what cannot be thought, and should guide us towards what can.

I certainly do not think such a position absurd or dishonest; but I think it paradoxical, and such paradoxes are only for the very clever. Religious stories are valued because they are thought to be in some sense true; liturgies are carried through because they are thought to put us in some relationship with a real world beyond; if religious language is used to back ethical prescriptions, it is because it is still felt to reflect metaphysical belief. The magic is gone from the Christmas stocking when the identity of Santa Claus is known; we may carry the ritual on for a few years for the nostalgia, but its days are numbered. Beliefs are not a dispensable superstructure, as a ship may sail on without its topmast. Smart's use of the word 'dimension' carries the same unfortunate suggestion, for our minds are used to three dimensions and boggle at four – surely, then, comes the idea, religion could do very well with five if it cannot have six. But the lives of Jesus and the saints spring from certain beliefs, held as convictions. Mother Teresa lives a life of heroic sanctity because she thinks that God wills her to, and the loss of her faith would not be comparable to removing gilt from gingerbread. Non-academic people – and that includes non-academic churchmen and non-academic saints – would feel that there is something bogus about saying prayers to a non-existent God, thanking him for an atonement he has not made, by the death of one who is not his Son; and that if the metaphysics are false and the Christian story is a myth in the pejorative sense, then no emotional response can spring naturally from it, and no ethic can be grounded in it. The church is strong at a residual level because people are reluctant to throw away the framework of beliefs by which they think they have hitherto lived their lives.

I cannot but sympathize with my friends who find it difficult to imagine the church, as the repository of our values, being replaced by the National Secular Society. But we cannot retain the church from motives of fear and nostalgia, which are no substitute for realism. If belief in God is not a valid option, then neither is Christianity a valid option. Man is an integral whole, his cognitive, affective and moral elements being bound together. There is no future for a church whose traditional beliefs are now to be entirely jettisoned, in the hope of retaining its morals and aspirations; and the attempt will seem to the plain believer to be a confidence trick. We have not lost our Christian vision of sympathy and compassion for all men by becoming humanists, and its grounding in religion was in any case dubious. Even if a future without the church is bleak, it is better to look bleakness in the eye, and see if we cannot construct a better basis for our love ethic. Maybe the future is a desert, but then our task is to recognize the fact and to try to make the desert bloom. Richard Martineau was fond of quoting Bishop Butler: 'Things and actions are what they are, and the consequences of them will be what they will be; why then should we wish to be deceived?' Homer taught us that life does not have a happy ending for most men; but we can still strive to live nobly.

2 Our Experience of God

John Hick

Michael has been a good friend – increasingly so – for some fifteen years; and no less since our all-day debate last November. I have long had the greatest respect both for his lucid intellect and for his personal integrity – which latter has led him to leave the priesthood, after so many years of faithful service, because he has ceased to believe in the reality of God. I had indeed long wondered whether his belief was adequately based; for he always expressed both an incomprehension of religious experience and a sympathy for the Farrer-type of theology which, while highly subtle and elusive, apparently involved the idea of providential divine interventions in human affairs. Such a combination could well lead to agnosticism. My hope, of course, is that the agnosticism will itself be a phase in the larger voyage of the *Fram*, an instance of *reculer pour mieux sauter*. At any rate, I now have to indicate why I, and many others, *do* believe in the reality of God.

1. I am going to take up one after another a number of points, the first of which concerns the word 'God'. This word points in the direction of a transcendent reality, or supposed reality, but points from a number of different angles in that it is used by different people in a wide overlapping range of ways. One person thinks of God as a great supernatural person, another as the infinite transpersonal Ground of all Being, or as the creative Spirit; to one God is the loving heavenly Father, to another the stern Judge. To one God is known as the Father of Jesus Christ, to another as the Yahweh of Israel, to another as Allah of the Quranic revelation. In short, 'God' is not used in just one identical way but in a whole family of ways. If I may quote from a believer in God from outside our immediate Christian household of faith, Gandhi said, 'The

contents of the richest word – God – are not the same to every one of us. They will vary with the experience of each.'[1] But at the same time all thoughtful believers in God, even whilst they each think of God partly in their own way, also insist that God is unlimited, and is the ultimate reality, exceeding the encompassing power of our finite minds and languages. God is greater than any human doctrine of God and exceeds our various human awarenesses of God. One can of course have a purely formal definition of God, for example as 'that than which no greater can be conceived'; but any concrete conception of God will be based on a particular human awareness of God, bound up with a particular human language and set of thought-forms.

2. My second point is that the question of the existence of God connects directly with the question of the nature of reality or the structure of the universe. If there is no God, we human animals have come into being within the blind evolution of the forms of matter, and will presently cease to exist both individually and as a species. God, good and evil, eternal life, are simply patterns in the brain of a transient form of life on the surface of one of the planets of a minor star on the periphery of a small galaxy in the virtual infinity of space and time. Millions of human beings, in generation after generation, have lived and died in tragic deprivation of adequate nourishment, of personal and political freedom, and of opportunities for cultural development and for creative activity; and if there is no God, this tragedy of deprivation and impoverishment is final and unredeemable. It is the sad fate of a large part of our human species to be casualties of a purposeless process, living and dying in intermittent pain and anxiety. This is the bleak picture painted by atheism. Now I do not of course say that because it is so bleak it must be false. But I do want to stress what a very different picture it is from that painted by the religions. In the God-centred picture, human life exists with the good purpose of God and that purpose will finally reach its fulfilment in a fullness of life and joy which are to us at present unimaginable. And if, beyond this present life, we do move towards such a fulfilment, we shall increasingly be conscious that we are doing so. The believer in God will have increasing confirmation of his belief, whilst the atheist will become increasingly aware that he had been mistaken. This factual and verifiable nature of the belief in God is a factor that I shall return to again later.

3. My third point concerns the philosophical arguments which have been offered over the centuries to prove the existence of God or to establish the probability of divine existence. These arguments are endlessly interesting, and are as live matters of philosophical discussion today as perhaps at any time in the past. But my own view – with which Michael will, I am sure, agree, although not everyone else will – is that none of these arguments actually proves the reality of God. That is to say, none of them is able to start from universally accepted premises and then show that it is irrational to accept these premises without believing in the existence of God. I would only add that the same is true with regard to all other matters of fact. The only conclusions that we can prove by strict logical demonstration concern the relations between ideas, not matters of fact and existence. We know about matters of fact and existence basically by observation, or experience, and not by philosophical arguments; and this applies also in the case of God. But the philosophical arguments do nevertheless, I think, serve an important purpose. They show the explanatory power of the concept of God by formulating fundamental questions to which the existence of God would constitute an intellectually satisfying answer. In this way they open the door to rational belief in God. But having opened the door they cannot, by themselves, propel anyone through it. They present the idea of God as a real possibility. But living religious belief is not merely the acknowledgment of this possibility. It is life lived in relation to a reality in which being and value are one and which impinges upon us, so that we cannot but believe it to be there.

4. And so we come, fourth, to experience in general, on the way to religious experience in particular. By an experience we mean a modification of consciousness. So long as we are conscious, our experience constitutes a continuous stream, the contents of which are partly supplied by external reality impinging upon us, and partly by internal factors, deliberate reasonings, and thoughts and feelings which come to the surface of consciousness from within our own minds. We are concerned here with those aspects or moments of our experience which seem to us to be caused by the impact of reality outside us. In the technical language of the phenomenologists this is 'intentional' experience, or in another terminology, which I shall use here, it is 'apparently cognitive' experience. Thus my present experience of the presence of the

desk on which my script is lying is an example of an apparently cognitive experience. For it seems to me that the desk is impinging upon me so as to cause the contents of my consciousness to be different from what they would be if there were no desk there. And my thus experiencing its presence is my reason for believing that the desk exists. For we normally trust our apparently cognitive experience, even though we also know that there are such occurrences as hallucinations, in which one's apparently cognitive experience is not caused by external realities but by purely internal factors. The basic principle on which we work is that it is reasonable for us to accept as veridical what seems to be an experience of some aspect of reality outside us, *unless* we have some reason to doubt it. You are of course free to doubt your experience, in general or in detail, not for any particular reason but simply because it is always in principle capable of being doubted. However, if you fall into that pit of general scepticism you will find that there is no rational ladder by which to climb out again. There is no way of *proving* even the reality of our physical environment. And one of the lessons of European philosophy since Descartes has been that it is more rational not to fall into that bottomless scepticism in the first place. It is perfectly reasonable and sane for us to trust our experience as generally cognitive of reality except when we have some reason to doubt it; and the mere theoretical possibility that any or all of it may be illusory does not count as a reason to doubt it. I would suggest that this principle applies generally to apparently cognitive experience, including religious experience.

5. What then is religious experience, or more precisely, since this is what we are concerned with today, what is theistic (i.e. God-related) religious experience? I shall give some concrete examples in a minute. But first a general philosophical account.

In the familiar case of seeing the desk I undergo a particular form of experience, i.e. a modification of my consciousness, which I describe as 'seeing the desk'. And having eschewed general scepticism, what we assume to be happening is that this modification of my consciousness is caused by the presence of the desk, whose nature is such that, when I am in the right position in relation to it, it impinges upon me and causes this kind of modification to occur in my stream of consciousness. It is also of course the case that, as we have already noted, experience is not infallible, so that it is possible that sometimes when people have the experience which is described as 'seeing a desk' they are being deluded because there is in fact no desk there. Now likewise many people report various forms of experience, or modifications of consciousness, which they describe in religious language, as, for example, experiencing the presence of God, or as the experiencing of existing in God's presence. And what, on the same principle, they assume to be happening is that these modifications to human consciousness are being caused by the reality and presence of God. There is an impact and pressure of the divine presence upon the human spirit, one's consciousness of which is one's experience of God. But once again, experience is not infallible. It is possible that the entire dimension of human experience is delusory. And so the question before us is: Is it or is it not reasonable, rational, sane, for the religious person to trust his or her own religious experience, together with that of the historical stream, and the present community of experiencers, within which it has occurred?

But let us ask first how this kind of impact and pressure of the divine reality upon human consciousness might possibly take place. The situation does not seem to be that God arbitrarily compels someone to become aware of him, even though once someone *is* aware of God the awareness often does have a powerful and indubitable quality. But there seems to be an essential human contribution to the encounter, in the form of a personal openness and a willingness to exist consciously in the divine presence. Such openness and willingness is always a matter of degree, so that as a result there are many levels of intensity of theistic religious experience. But as to *how* spirit affects spirit, or mind affects mind, this is ultimately as unknown to us as how matter affects matter, or indeed how matter affects mind. We observe what we call cause and effect in the physical world. That is to say, we observe that the natural order is such that when A happens B happens. But we cannot go beyond more and more detailed regularities of this kind, which we call laws of nature. And it is the same with mental causation. We do have in parapsychology a growing body of observations of the apparently direct influence of mind on mind; but we have not got far towards formulating the laws – that is, the observable regularities – of this kind of causation. And when we turn to the supposed impact of the divine Spirit upon our human consciousnesses, all that we can say is that it apparently happens. To some extent William James, in his *Varieties of Religious Experience*,

35

and others since him, have contributed to the study of the human conditions under which it happens; but the systematic study of religious experience is still only in its infancy.

6. Next, I must remind you of my first point and now extend it somewhat. If a limitless divine reality confronts and surrounds us, we may reasonably expect that we finite human creatures will both conceive of it and experience it in all manner of partial, inadequate and perhaps distorted ways. Religious experience will accordingly be various, taking many forms, and always including a human contribution which influences the specific form that it takes on a particular occasion. In other words, there may well be an element of human projection mixed with the all-important element of divine presence and pressure. Indeed when we look at the history of religions we have to conclude that there undoubtedly *is* such a human element. For the pressure and impact of God is being felt through our human states of mind, which may be in so many ways resistant or sensitive to the divine presence. I shall give you presently some examples of what I regard as the central kind of theistic experience, namely the sense of the presence of God. But let us remember that there are also the experiences of someone like the notorious Jim Jones, the charismatic religious leader who was responsible for the horrible Jonestown, Guyana, massacre in 1978; and many other grossly distorted and aberrant perversions of religious awareness. Each of the great religious traditions, including Christianity, has in fact its criteria by which to distinguish between authentic and inauthentic forms of religious experience. The most basic criterion, common to all the great traditions, is ethical, based upon observation of the moral fruits in the experiencer's life; and by this criterion almost everybody would agree that the Jim Jones type of person was either mentally or morally deranged and was desperately deluded. Accepting the need for such discriminations, then, we are back at the basic question whether the realm of religious experience as a whole should or should not be regarded by those who participate in it as representing the effects within human consciousness of the reality and presence of God. I have already suggested that because all our knowledge of what there is and of how things are is ultimately based upon our own experience and upon the experience of other people, it must be rational for us to trust our experience, except when we have some reason to doubt it. I now want to add that the

fact that we make discriminations, trying to distinguish between genuine and false moments of religious experience, is not itself a reason to doubt the veridical character of this dimension of human experience as a whole. Nor does the fact that there are borderline cases when it is very difficult to decide whether they are genuine or not, and when different people may judge differently, entail that religious experience as a whole is delusory. It may still be the case that through the manifold hindrances and distortions operating at our human end of the process there is nevertheless a real presence and pressure of the divine Spirit upon the human spirit, causing the modifications of our consciousness which we then correctly describe as the experience of existing in the presence of God.

And so we must free ourselves from any assumption that if there is a divine reality whose presence impinges upon our human consciousnesses, the effect of that impingement must always take the same form, or that all the forms must be of equal value, or that there cannot be grave misperceptions and misunderstandings of God as well as a wide range of variously correct perceptions and understandings. We must also, I believe, accept that the experience of existing in God's presence will always be mixed, in the individual's own consciousness, and in the ways in which it is articulated, with the body of his or her acquired beliefs, both about God and about the world.

As a very rough analogy for this situation, imagine a group of people standing among the foothills of a huge Himalayan mountain, which towers above them into the mists, its upper reaches hidden from their view, though occasionally through the swirling mists they catch a glimpse of the mighty peaks far above them. They have heard different reports from explorers who in the past have climbed a certain distance up the mountain by different routes, and from these reports they have received different impressions of the mountain's shape and character. Further, they may respond emotionally in rather different ways, according to their own inner states and needs, one feeling awed and overwhelmed by the mountain's sheer majesty and power, another feeling exhilarated and liberated by its purity and beauty, and so on. Thus they all perceive it and think of it somewhat differently. And amidst this variety of thoughts and perceptions there is undoubtedly an admixture of error, elements of mistaken thinking and misperceiving. But nevertheless when we ask the basic question whether there is a real mountain there, they will quite reasonably and properly be completely convinced that there is. They will be relying on the mutually reinforcing effects of the accumulated reports of others both now and in the past, and of their own more limited personal observations. And my suggestion is that it is perfectly rational, sane, sensible and appropriate for them to do this.

7. Now it is time for some specific examples of theistic (that is, God-related) religious experiences. There are both what the psychologist Abraham Maslow calls 'peak experiences', which occur at some particular time and which are very striking and such that people are likely to remember them for the rest of their lives; and also (and more importantly for most people) the ordinary low-intensity, relatively undramatic religious dimension of some of the moments of quite ordinary life.

Let us begin with the peaks, and indeed with the very rare phenomenon of life lived on a more or less continuous peak or plateau of powerful and compelling awareness of the reality and presence of God. The most intense and continuous such awareness known to us within the Christian tradition is that of Jesus himself. He seems to have been conscious all the time of the presence of God as the most real of all realities. God, the heavenly Father to whom he spoke in prayer, in whose name he healed and pronounced forgiveness, and about whom he taught, was as real to him as the people he was talking to, or as the hills and Lake of Galilee. I presume that it would have seemed as absurd to him to suppose that God does not exist as to suppose that Nazareth does not exist or that his disciples did not exist. In other words, he seems to have lived more or less continuously on the heights of religious awareness. And as has often been the case, the powerful contagion of a compelling religious experience drew others into his own consciousness of God, a consciousness which, when he was no longer with them, they called the experience of the Holy Spirit.

Now we have to ask whether it was reasonable for Jesus to believe wholeheartedly in the heavenly Father whose reality and presence he seemed to be experiencing in this way. For clearly it is both possible that this apparently cognitive experience was delusory and also possible that the experience was authentically cognitive, representing the impact upon his consciousness of a divine reality and presence. I suggest that it is entirely reasonable, rational and sane for the person who has this kind of immensely powerful and compelling sense of the presence of God to trust his or her own experience as veridical and to proceed to live and to believe on the basis of it. To reject so pervasive and powerful a form of experience would be tantamount to doubting one's own sanity. It would be a kind of cognitive suicide. And for someone who has the experience of existing in the presence of God, over prolonged periods of time, in that overwhelmingly impressive way, not only is it rational to believe in the reality of God but it would be irrational not to.

Now some examples of lesser peak experiences. The Bible is full of them; but I prefer to come nearer to our own time, and indeed right into our own time, by drawing examples from two modern collections of religious experience reports. One of my sources is that great classic *The Varieties of Religious Experience* by William James, who made use of the psychologist Edwin Starbuck's collection, made in the United States at the end of the last century. My other source is the contemporary collection still being made by the Religious Experience Research Unit at Oxford, which was founded in 1969 by the distinguished Oxford zoologist, Professor Sir Alister Hardy. Part of the Research Unit's material has been published in a series of books, and I shall be taking cases mainly from one of these volumes, *A Sense of Presence* by Timothy Beardsworth. But first from William James' collection:

There was not a mere consciousness of something there, but fused in the central happiness of it, a startling awareness of some ineffable good. Not vague either, not like the emotional effect of some poem, or scene, or blossom, or music, but the sure knowledge of the close presence of a sort of mighty person, and after it went, the memory persisted as the one perception of reality. Everything else might be a dream, but not that.[2]

The second, also written in rather Victorian prose, is as follows:

I remember the night, and almost the very spot on the hill-top, where my soul opened out, as it were, into the Infinite, and there was a rushing together of the two worlds, the inner and the outer. . . I stood alone with Him who had made me, and all

39

the beauty of the world, and love, and sorrow, and even temptation. I did not seek Him, but felt the perfect unison of my spirit with His. The ordinary sense of things around me faded. For the moment nothing but the ineffable joy and exultation remained. It is impossible fully to describe the experience. . . The darkness held a presence that was all the more felt because it was not seen. I could not any more have doubted that *He* was there than that I was. Indeed, I felt myself to be, if possible, the less real of the two.[3]

The next two are taken from Beardsworth's book of contemporary reports:

The whole room seemed to be filled by an overwhelming Presence, and I was filled with an absolute peace. I even looked up at the empty place beside my chair, seeing nothing, but aware that all was well.[4]

Again:

There was no sensible vision, but the room was filled by a Presence which in a strange way was both about me and within me. I was overwhelmingly possessed by Someone who was not myself, and yet I felt I was more myself than I had ever been before.[5]

Here, once again, we have to ask: should people who undergo such experiences as these dismiss them as some kind of delusion, and perhaps fear for their own mental health, or should they accept them with gratitude as the immensely enhancing touch of the divine reality upon them? At this point I must declare an interest, as the lawyers say; for I am one of the many people who are deluded if such experiences are delusory.

An experience of this kind which I cannot forget, even though it happened forty-two years ago now, occurred – of all places – on the top deck of a bus in the middle of the city of Hull, when I was a law student at University College, Hull. As everyone will be very conscious who can themselves remember such a moment, all descriptions are inadequate. But it was as though the skies opened up and light poured down and filled me with a sense of overflowing joy in response to an immense transcendent goodness and love. I remember that I couldn't help smiling broadly – smiling back, as

40

it were, at God – though if any of the other passengers were looking they must have thought that I was a lunatic, grinning at nothing. And there have been a number of less intense, usually much less intense, moments from time to time, varying from a background sense to a momentarily more specific sense of existing in the unseen presence of God.

8. Now an observation about the phenomenology of such experiences as these. They are importantly different from what you might call spooky or eerie experiences, encounters with the supernatural, magic, hauntings, ghosts, poltergeists and the like. What distinguishes the religious experience from all this is the unity of ultimacy and value. The presence that is felt is not experienced as a particular finite entity, but as cosmic and ultimate. And it is not experienced as value neutral but as the reality in which being and value are one. Thus the contact with this presence creates joy and awe. The experience is not spooky, but awe-inspiring, not frightening but nevertheless deeply impressive. It would, I think, be impossible for such an experience not to stir deep emotions. Further, it is profoundly enhancing, having a very positive aspect, releasing goodwill and love towards others. Let me at this point quote just one more account, this time taken from Sir Alister Hardy's book *The Spiritual Nature of Man*. The place was a railway carriage in a stationary train in Vauxhall Station in London:

> For a few seconds only, I suppose, the whole compartment was filled with light. This is the only way I know in which to describe the moment, for there was nothing to *see* at all. I felt caught up into some tremendous sense of being within a loving, triumphant and shining purpose. . . A most curious, but overwhelming sense possessed me and filled me with ecstasy. I felt that all was well for mankind – how poor the words seem! The word 'well' is so poverty-stricken. Beauty, music, joy, love immeasurable and a glory unspeakable, all this they would inherit. . . An indescribable joy possessed me. . . All this happened over fifty years ago but even now I can see myself in the corner of that dingy, third-class compartment with the feeble lights of inverted gas mantles overhead and the Vauxhall Station platform outside with milk cans standing there. In a few moments the glory departed – all but one curious lingering feeling. I loved every-

body in that compartment. It sounds silly now, and indeed I blush to write it, but at that moment I think I would have died for any one of the people in that compartment.[6]

Now all of these reports – and many hundreds of others that are available – present the same question. Clearly the experiences which they describe *could* all be hallucinatory, telling us something about the person who has the experience but nothing about the nature of reality and the meaning of our existence. Or again they *could* be descriptions of different effects within different human consciousnesses at different times and in different circumstances of the presence and pressure of the divine reality which we call God.

But before tackling that question head on let us come to what I called the low-intensity, relatively undramatic religious dimension of some of the moments of ordinary life. And let me say first that these are continuous with the so-called peak experiences. The peak experiences are not utterly different in kind from more humdrum forms of religious experience, but are high-points within a continuum. Those who have been fortunate enough to undergo a relatively peak experience are not special people; they do not constitute any kind of spiritual elite; they are just unaccountably lucky to have seen the veil of ordinary consciousness partially lifted for a moment. But the more common experiential basis of faith is of a much less striking kind. For example, many people can report moments when the idea of God, the thought of God, takes on a special power and intensity, a strong sense of reality. Again many people can report moments whilst praying, or whilst receiving communion, or whilst meditating, or when reading the Bible, or listening to the lesson in church, when they have been seized by a sense of the reality and environing presence of God – perhaps in the form of a grateful sense of God's goodness to them, or of God's forgiveness or acceptance, or again of God's challenging claim upon their lives, leading them to do or refrain from doing some particular thing. Such moments may occur in church; and indeed a liturgy is, or should be, designed to function as a trigger of religious experience. But for many people the occasional moments when life takes on a religious dimension are not in church but in some natural setting that already has what we might call a cosmic dimension, as when we look up into the infinity of a starry night, or watch the endless waves of the sea, or gaze at the long vistas of a mountain scene. Such moments may also function as triggers of religious experience. They may open one's consciousness to the transcendent. So also may the sense, which many people have experienced, of the sheer contingency of our existence. Yet another range of situations the experience of which can take on a religious dimension is that of a moral claim upon one's life, including the contemporary consciousness of a demand to work for the welfare of humanity in face of the threats of nuclear destruction, environmental disaster, world poverty, racism, the suppression of human freedom. As in the case of the Hebrew prophets of old, the powerfully felt obligation to seek justice and peace can be experienced as the claim of God upon one's life. Indeed I think we have to say that all manner of situations – perhaps in principle *any* situation – *may* function as what Ian Ramsey called a 'disclosure situation' in which, as he used to say, the penny drops, the ice breaks and the idea of God or of the transcendent takes on a compelling power and authority.

Here then is part at least of the range of the forms of religious experience. And I want to stress that when we find ourselves experiencing in any of these ways, whether of high or low intensity, we are not the first persons to do so; we are not isolated individuals undergoing some peculiar experience of our own. We are participating in a vast field or continuum of religious experience which goes back through the centuries and indeed millennia, with distinctive threads or streams running through it – the particular stream which provides the characteristic forms which our own religious experience takes being the Christian tradition. It would be one thing for you to have some momentary experience of your own, you being the only person in the world to have had that kind of experience, but a very different thing for you to participate, even in a small way, in a dimension of human experience which encircles the globe and runs through all human history.

9. Now at last we come to the sixty-four thousand dollar question of the validity or trustworthiness of religious experience. Let me say at once that such experiences do not *prove* the existence of God. As I have already indicated several times, it is theoretically possible (or in a more technical phrase, logically possible) that this entire realm of experience is delusory or hallucinatory, simply a human projection, and not in any way or degree a result of the

43

presence of a greater divine reality. I want to get this basic point entirely clear, because otherwise our debate might take the un-profitable form of my referring to various instances of experiences which seem to be experiences of the presence of God, and Michael replying, 'Yes, of course these experiences occur, but may they not nevertheless all be delusory, a kind of self-induced waking dream?' Our debate will be more profitable if we can start from the agreed position that, looked at entirely neutrally and objectively, this realm of experience *may* be delusory and *may* be a genuine awareness of the presence of a divine reality; and that the question before us is what it is most reasonable for us to believe about it. And immediately we have to distinguish between, on the one hand, the question facing the person who has not (as of now, at any rate) participated in the sense of the presence of God, and who accordingly does not know what this experience is, and on the other hand the question facing the person who *has* participated in this form of experience even if only, it may be, to a very slight extent. I do not want to claim that the first group of people, who have no first-hand knowledge of what religious experience is, ought to believe in the reality of God on the basis of the reports of other people. Rather, it would seem to me that one who does not participate at all in the field of religious experience should reserve judgment. He should say to himself: these people talk of a form of experience in which I have not participated, but which if it is genuine points to the reality of a divine being. Clearly, they may very well all be deluding themselves. But then again they may not. So I shall remain agnostic. This, it appears to me, is the rational stance for the non-religious person to take; and I hope that it will become evident that this is Michael's stance.

But what should those who *do* participate in some degree in theistic religious experience make of their own experience and the wider experience of which theirs is a part? Is it proper for them to trust their own experience, together with the more powerful experiences of others within their own religious community, regarding this as generally cognitive of reality?

10. My concluding point is that it is totally reasonable and rational for the religious person, looking at the whole continuum of religious experience and participating in one's own small way in that continuum, to proceed to live and to form beliefs on the basis of it. Here I want to adapt an argument from William James'

famous essay 'The Will to Believe', an essay which he himself recognized should have been called 'The Right to Believe'. I say adapt, because I think that James made one major wrong move in the course of his argument, a wrong move which can however be rectified; and I shall put the argument now in its amended form.

The starting point is the fact that we are living in a situation of theoretic ambiguity. The universe is capable of being construed either religiously or naturalistically. There is the possibility not only of complete and consistent religious interpretations of it, but also of complete and consistent naturalistic interpretations of it. And these are not – this, you may remember, was my second point – merely optional subjective views, but are such that one type of interpretation must in fact be essentially correct and the other essentially incorrect. That is to say, the actual structure of the universe, including its future development through time, will either turn out to express a creative divine purpose or not to express any such purpose.

Now William James argued that in such a situation, when the matter at issue is enormously important to us, we have the right, if we feel so drawn, to commit ourselves to the religious option. The way in which he put it was that, either way, we are running a tremendous risk. For whether we like it or not, we have to proceed, in both belief and life, either on the basis that the religious picture of the universe is essentially true or on the basis that a naturalistic picture is essentially true. There is no neutral position between these two alternatives; the choice is, as James put it, a forced option. For if the religious interpretation of the universe is correct it is only by adopting it and living it out that one can hope progessively to relate oneself to and thus be changed by the divine reality. On the other hand, if the naturalistic interpretation is correct, the religious option can only lead us into error and delusion. Thus we run an unavoidable risk whichever option we choose. The possible gain is that of living in terms of reality, and the possible loss is that of living in delusion. James argues that in such a situation it is entirely rational for us to follow the prompting of our instincts and desires. It is at this point, it seems to me, that he makes his only wrong move. It is not enough that we *desire* the religious option to be true. But if our reason for opting for it is that it accords with our own experience, with religious experience as the clinching factor, then it seems to me that James' argument is valid and persuasive. If in the existing situation of theoretic ambiguity a person experiences life religiously, that person is rationally entitled to trust his or her religious experience, and to proceed to believe and to live on the basis of it.

And so to conclude. There is a vast continuum of forms and degrees of theistic religious experience, ranging from the powerful and continuous sense of God's presence, experienced by the great saints, to a very ordinary and fleeting sense of the reality of God experienced by ordinary people in moments of prayer and meditation, or when reading the scriptures, or when confronted with the vastness and mystery of the universe, or when conscious of the contingency of existence, or contemplating the idea of God, or when aware of a transcendent claim upon one's life, or in some other context. And within this wide continuum there are also, for a number of people at least, peak experiences, unforgettably vivid and moving moments of awareness of being in God's unseen presence. And through one's own form of religious experiencing, however intense or however faint, however continuous or however occasional and rare, one is linked to and part of a great history of religious experience. One is not alone in this matter, but a member of a great company. For some that company is the Christian church or the Jewish race or the Muslim *ummah*, down the ages and today; and for some it is the world-wide multitude of those who have experienced and do experience our human life as being lived in the universal presence of God.

Now it is theoretically possible that this whole dimension of human experience is delusory. It is also no less possible that through it we are being affected by the reality and presence of a transcendent creative power, which confronts us as good and gracious, and whose reality gives us profound joy, releasing new possibilities within us. In this situation, a situation of what I have called theoretic ambiguity, it matters enormously whether we respond to the divine presence so as to be able to be more and more affected by it, or reject it as illusory and thus so far as we can cut ourselves off from it. And my claim is that in this situation it is entirely reasonable, rational, appropriate and sane for us to make the positive response, the response of faith, trusting our own experience together with that of the fellowship of believers and of the saints and the great servants of God, and to proceed to try both to live and believe on the basis of this dimension of our existence.

3   How Dependable is Experience?
Michael Goulder

The nub of Professor Hick's argument – or John, as I shall call him, for he is an old and valued friend – is the comparability of our experience of God with our experience of the world. He is surely right to urge us to trust our experience of this world unless there is reason to doubt it, and he is surely right also to insist that what seem to be experiences of God should be treated in exactly the same way as what seem to be experiences of this world. Nevertheless, the parallel leaves the reader feeling slightly ill at ease; for surely the rider 'unless there is reason to doubt it' will affect some classes of this-worldly experience more than others, and these classes may most closely resemble the experiences of God.

In general, our this-worldly experiences are supported by what we may call evidence – that is, outward, visible, public checks suggesting that we have got it right. We are not much in doubt over experiencing desks: if nervous of hallucination we may put out a hand and touch them. The less clear the evidence, the more we feel reason to doubt the experience. 'Charming people, the Browns,' I say to my wife as we leave the party. 'What made you think that?' she replies, dangerously. 'Well,' I say, 'John Brown seemed very interested in my theory of the psalms, and I thought Susan was sweet.' 'You think all pretty women are sweet, my love', comes the twinkling answer, 'and John Brown is a greasy man who wants you to give him a job.' We have experienced the Browns, but differently from the same evidence: but at least here we have the smiles and looks of concentration to go by.

There are no smiles or looks of concentration with God; and it is this that makes it so difficult to evaluate claims of awareness of his presence. But certainly we can say that as we take away the

47

evidence more and more completely in different human experiences, we feel less and less confident that we can call it rational to trust them. The Browns were sending out signals, whether genuine or meretricious; but there are occasions when it is in question whether signals are being sent out at all. Suppose you have a friend who is in love with a young woman, and he is persuaded that his passion is returned. His confidence rests on the fact that he has invited her out to dinner, and she has accepted. But you know your friend to be good company, and a bon viveur, and also pressing in invitations: it may seem to you that she had little option, quite apart from other possible reasons for accepting. The next day his confidence is confirmed: she has accepted a volume of poetry. Perhaps, you think; but then again she could hardly decline. A visit to her home has finally settled the matter, you are assured: while she was out of the room he glanced at the book, and she had made a pencil mark against a love poem. Now at this point you may feel that your friendship imposes a duty on you. You cannot of course know whether the young lady feels for your friend or not; but it may be manifestly clear to you by now that his confidence rests entirely upon wishful thinking. It may seem suitable to you therefore to warn your friend not to hope too highly unless he has more to go on than he has told you. For – and here is the essence of the matter – his experience of her feeling affection for him, without proper evidence, is irrational.

But what if there were no sign of the Browns, or of the young lady at all? For that is the situation with God. A distasteful but apposite illustration comes to mind. Some years ago the then Minister of Defence was having an extramarital affair, and the room in which this was being conducted contained a large mirror, so made that it was possible to see through it from the far side. This arrangement permitted a certain doctor to watch all that happened without being perceived. Now we can imagine the Minister saying, 'I have an uncomfortable feeling that we are being watched', and if pressed he might say, 'I don't know what it is – that mirror gives me the creeps.' Often people may correctly sense the presence of an unwanted stranger – a burglar perhaps – and not be able to put their finger on what it is that has alerted them. But if, after due pressing, drawing the curtains, etc., there is no substance given to such 'sensing a presence', we should feel it proper to dismiss it. If someone tells us that he never loses the sense of being followed by a sinister oriental, we should advise him to see a psychiatrist. If a man tells us that he means to act, as he has the experience of his neighbour wanting to murder him, but has no evidence, we may mention him to the police. Claims of experience in this world without evidence are irrational.

But are there not instances in everyday life when people really do experience things without any evidence, and turn out to be right? The fact that some people are paranoid or loony does not give us the right to suppose that John is paranoid or loony; and indeed that would be a most implausible hypothesis.

Perhaps we may think of people separated from those whom they love, and who say that they have vivid feelings of relationships for which there can be no possible evidence; and afterwards these claims have turned out to be true. A woman I knew in Oswestry told me of two sudden feelings of constriction which she had while alone one evening with her daughter. She went out to the kitchen during these, and began to cry, fearing that some harm had befallen her absent husband. Soon afterwards a phone call announced his death, ten minutes after a heart attack. This is not quite an instance of awareness of a presence, but there certainly are impressive cases of telepathy, experiences without accompanying evidence. Or perhaps we know of couples who have been separated by war, or in prisoner-of-war camps, and the man may tell his fellow soldiers that the thing that keeps him going is his certainty that his wife or girl friend is thinking about him; and when the great reunion takes place, he finds that she had indeed been faithful, and has visited his family often and spoken about him. Is not this a more friendly instance of an unevidenced experience which later turns out to be true? Of course, as John will be quick to add, such claims may also sometimes turn out to be false; but then we cannot promise ourselves that our faith in God will turn out to be true, only that it is rational to trust our experience of his presence, there being no adequate reason to the contrary.

I am afraid, however, that instances of this kind do not bear out John's claim at all: for the whole point about them is that they are based upon plenty of evidence. Husbands and wives, and even soldiers and their girl friends, may know each other extremely well. We do not understand the mechanism of telepathy, but clearly in a lifetime of living together they may develop a great sensitivity to each other's feelings, even in absence. A young man may know that his girl really cares for him, and that she has a dependable character, even if he has known her for only three months. This is not at all the sort of experience John is speaking of, because with his theology God has never taken any of those initiatives which enable husband and wife to feel they know each other. John's God never leaves a bunch of roses, or washes our shirt when we are not looking.

It is this absence of supporting outward and visible signs which vitiates John's analogy of the mountain. Despite the swirling mists, etc., it is entirely rational for the foothill dwellers to posit the existence of Kanchenjunga, for they have (a) occasional glimpses of it on clear days, and (b) reports of mountaineers. The occasional glimpses obviously do not quite apply with God, for glimpses of mountains are public experiences, so that a man will say to his companion, 'Look!' while 'glimpses' of God, however powerfully felt, are private experiences. The latter would be better compared to moments of vision of a scientist where, beyond the 'foothills' of laboratory experiments, he may 'glimpse the mountain' of the benzine ring, or some sudden massive insight into reality. I will return in a moment to the reports of the mountaineers, but the primary point I wish to establish may be recapitulated thus. John's central line of argument is this:

It is rational to trust experience, unless there is reason to doubt it. Experience of God should be treated like this-worldly experience. Therefore it is rational to trust experience of God unless there is reason to doubt it.

This does not work, because we only think it rational to trust our this-worldly experience normally when there are agreed, public, outward and visible signs to bear it out. It is precisely where such evidence is lacking that we take such claims of experience to be irrational.

But what are we to say of the mountaineers' reports'? Surely it would be harsh to accuse Jesus, for example, of irrationality in the light of his (presumed) experience? Indeed it would: but then what is rational in one century is not necessarily rational in another. John represents the difference between the faith of Jesus and that of the ordinary Christian today as if it were one of 'level', high and low, or of clarity of experience: Jesus experienced God more or less continuously, as vividly real, more real than the hills, etc., while the ordinary Christian's experience is patchy, and liable to doubt. But this way of stating the difference seems to me very misleading. If we could bring Jesus in a time machine here to us today, and persuade him that we were serious in asking whether it is rational to believe in God, and if so, why he believed in God, I suppose he would say something like this:

'I find it amazing that anyone could doubt the most obvious fact that there is, but since you ask me, I will tell you. How could there not be a God, when the world is here which he created out of nothing six thousand years ago? You can tell by the regularity of seed-time and harvest, which would never come regularly unless God had made a covenant with Noah. How could the people of Israel be here, unless God had divided the Red Sea to bring them out of Egypt, and given them the Land? Where did the Law come from, which is read every sabbath, unless God had given it to us on Sinai? And besides, I know my heavenly Father in daily prayer. I know that prayer is real, because when I ask, fantastic healings happen all the time. My relationship with Him is the most real thing in my life. I am in a special relationship with Him that others do not share: I am his Son, and he calls me to costly obedience each day, and maybe to a painful death one day.'

Jesus' faith, in other words, rested on two bases, which made it wholly rational. First he shared with his entire community a broad web of interrelated beliefs, for each of which there was outward and visible evidence: the world, the harvest, the people, the Land, the scriptures, etc. To have rejected such overwhelming evidence would have been the act of a lunatic; indeed, it is difficult to see how even a lunatic could have leapt outside the world-view of his community. But this general background evidence was confirmed for Jesus by something more pressing still, his own charisma. It seemed to him that God's kingdom had begun to arrive, and the evidence for this cannot but have seemed irrefutable. Day after day he was effectively casting out demons, and healing multiple sickness – quite apart from drawing enormous crowds and enthusiastic disciples. In such circumstances he could do nothing else but read his life in the light of biblical revelation, and see himself as the long-promised Christ. His every step must have been experienced in the light of the will of his heavenly Father.

Such a brief exercise of the imagination should suffice to make clear the crucial difference between Jesus' faith and John (Hick)'s

51

faith. John's faith is based on 'experience' only: he doesn't think that God made a covenant with Noah, or that he divided the Red Sea, or that he delivered the Law to Moses, or that Jesus' miracles were miracles in the traditional sense, or that Jesus was God's Son or the Christ in the way those expressions were understood in the first century: even the creation he understands in a very sophisticated sense. I am not telling you these sobering facts in order to reveal to you the depth of John's unbelief. On the contrary, many theologians share John's position, and I think that by taking this option he has given the church a subtle line of defence. I tell you these things in order to make my distinction clear. Jesus' faith was based in part on his experience of God, and in part on a large variety of supporting evidence – the world, the land, the miracles, etc. These were a web of facts whose interpretation in his community was not liable to doubt, and which seemed to guarantee that the experience of God was real. Jesus held what we may call a red-blooded theology: his God did a lot of things, and you could see the results of his initiatives on every hand. I will not call John's theology bloodless, which would be pejorative, and I am trying to be fair: I will call it a driven-snow theology, because it leaves the world pure of any divine interference or manipulation. His God acts only by willing our good; and this action becomes effective only in so far as we respond to his impressive presence.

Just as John leaves out this enormously important outward and visible element of Jesus' experience, so does he with the early church. It is not a fair account of what happened to Peter and the others to refer to 'the powerful contagion of compelling experience' which led them after the crucifixion to speak of consciousness of the Holy Spirit. We cannot know exactly what happened at Pentecost, but it is clear that in the 50s Christians in Corinth experienced speaking with tongues, ecstatic visions, conviction that they understood such tongues, etc.; and that these regular features of worship must have gone back to some dramatic 'outpouring' in earlier days. Paul speaks also of miracles, healings and prophesying, which seems to mean inspired preaching. The Gospels refer to the Holy Spirit as speaking through Christians on trial for their faith: in the hour of need, quite inarticulate men could be heard testifying with courage and eloquence to their beliefs. St Luke tells us further in Acts that the church in the person of leaders like Stephen and Paul seemed to reproduce the whole pattern and character of Jesus' ministry and death. So here, the early church, like Jesus, had a vast web of factual evidence whose interpretation was not in doubt, which subtended its experience of the Holy Spirit. Here we are not dependent upon our unaided imaginations, for there are congregations of black Pentecostal Christians in many cities in this country whose experience of the Spirit (with accompanying evidence) is as clear as daylight, and leaves them in a state of complete and unshakable certainty. So here too, experience is accompanied by evidence, and is entirely rational, whether or not it is actually veridical.

The difficulty John faces with his 'mountaineers' reports' is that he holds the data on which they are based to be erroneous. 'Excuse me,' you say to the man in the waiting room, 'what time does the London train leave?' He looks up from his crossword: '10.14,' he says, after due consideration. 10.14 comes, and you wonder whether he was dependable after all. 'I am sorry to trouble you,' you resume, 'where did you get the information that the train was 10.14?' 'No trouble at all,' he replies, '10 across is "train" and 14 down is "London".' Will you still wait for the 10.14 notwithstanding? Pip, in *Great Expectations*, is given an expensive education by an unknown benefactor, whom he believes erroneously to be a wealthy but eccentric old lady in the neighbourhood. Naturally he imagines the old lady as caring for him, interested in his progress, and so on; he feels a sense of gratitude to her. Then one day he learns that this was an entire error: his benefactor is an escaped convict who has made good in Australia and who has returned his boyhood kindness in full measure. Surely we should think Pip quixotic if he insisted that, even without the supposed actions, he still felt that the old lady cared for him and was interested in him? Jesus and the early Christians experienced God as acting in certain ways; if, with John, we take it that they were mistaken in those interpretations, then surely the rational thing is to hold their experience of God in radical doubt also?

Of course it would be impossible for a large community of sane and intelligent people such as constitute the Christian church to keep their belief going if it were based on nothing but 'misexperience'. But experience does not arise without evidence. The Christian religion arises from evidences such as we have considered, and almost all Christians today have begun by believing at least the incarnation and the resurrection to be true in some

53

straightforward sense. From belief in these evidences follow experiences of conversion, salvation, sanctification, fellowship with God and the rest. By far the largest part of the church believes much more than this, and it is not surprising that experience attends belief. If you are told, whether as child or adult, that God gave his Son to die by crucifixion for your sins, and you believe it, you may expect to have certain feelings of horror, gratitude, awareness of the divine Thou, etc. But the evidence seems to the sophisticates of the church to be false evidence. Noah never lived; there never was an east wind that divided the Red Sea; Jesus was a 'mere' man who responded uniquely to the loving will of God; his body never left the tomb. In this way they have sawn off the branch that they have been sitting on. Their faith is the grin without the Cheshire Cat.

I do not think that John can reasonably reply to this attack, 'The demand for evidence is out of place. In the eighteenth century men looked for miracles breaking the laws of nature, fulfilments of prophecy, and so on. Today it is widely agreed that such expectations of finding independent support for our religious faith were misguided.' For one thing, it is not at all widely agreed that experience alone is enough. Karl Barth and Emil Brunner, to name but two twentieth-century theologians, believed the incarnation to be God's testimony to himself; and Wolfhart Pannenberg believes the same of the empty tomb.[1] The whole situation changes with them, because the 'mountaineers' reports' are then seen as in some vital aspect true. But even if they were all as sceptical as John, it would still not affect the force of my argument. If we think claims of experience in this world to be irrational in the absence of supporting evidence, then claims of experience of God are irrational also in the absence of supporting evidence; and it is quite immaterial to this judgment if a particular theology has defined such evidence out of possibility.

It would be open to John to drop the comparison with experience in this world, and to assert that religious experience was *sui generis*, but so compelling that those who have any awareness of God cannot rationally reject it. The degree of compellingness of different experiences of God is in fact a problem for John, with which he grapples in Chapter 2. For if we are to treat private experiences as veridical in the same sort of way we treat public experiences of desks, etc., they need to be pretty impressive. No one says, 'I think I saw a ghost last night': to treat a ghost-experience seriously we need a lot of convincing, preferably with stopped clocks and circumstantial detail. But then, as John concedes, most actual religious experience is rather 'low-level'. At the time, perhaps, the moment at the communion rail, or the clearly perceived ethical challenge, were felt as an awareness of the transcendent; in later years we wonder if that was right. Perhaps we were going through a romantic period, or were under the influence of a priest, or a friend, and just 'saw it like that'. So 'low-level' experiences need, for confidence, to be anchored in much more impressive, coercive experiences, like those of Jesus. 'God . . . was as real to him as the people he was talking to. . . It would have seemed as *absurd* to him to suppose that God does not exist as to suppose that Nazareth does not exist. . . It is entirely reasonable, rational, sane for the person who has this *immensely powerful and compelling* sense of the presence of God to trust his or her own experience as veridical. . . To reject *so pervasive and powerful* a form of experience would be tantamount to doubting one's own sanity' (see pp. 38f. above; my italics).

Jesus thus occupies a crucial place in John's argument, for John needs an instance of religious experience which covers three requirements: (a) it must be of a person of transparent goodness, not like Jim Jones; (b) it must be of someone with whom the reader can feel some natural affinity, so that his own 'low-level' experience (if any) may be linked on without strain; and (c) it must be sufficiently powerful, pervasive, compelling, etc., that it would be absurd not to trust it. In a 'Christian' community, Jesus is the obvious person to take. I have already objected that Jesus' experience was of a God who healed disease, raised the dead, and so on, so that both the reality and the character of God seemed to be given to him by events past and present. John looks at experience another way: he sees Jesus as experiencing God direct, except that that experience is filtered through, and distorted by, a screen of his own, and his community's beliefs. He really did experience the one, eternal, all-loving Ultimate, but he knew him through the embroidered muslin curtain of contemporary Jewish belief, the embroidery obstructing the pure experience. Mine seems to me the more natural view, but I have to allow that John's is possible.

But even so, there seems to be a major contradiction. For if we are to accept Jesus' experience of the transcendent as being so compelling that it would be absurd not to trust it, we cannot also think it to be wrong in some major area. But Jesus did not experience only his heavenly Father as transcending his everyday world: he also experienced the world of demons. It is difficult, therefore, to escape from the dilemma: if Jesus' experience of the transcendent is to be allowed as too powerful to be refused, then we must accept that it is absurd not to trust his experience of demons as well as of God. But John does not believe in demons! The normal hope of escaping the difficulty is to argue that demons were a *hypothesis*, a part of the contemporary world-view of the first century, by which one *explained* madness, epilepsy, squalls, moral weakness, etc. God was not a hypothesis, but an *experienced* reality. But even a casual glance at a few of the Gospel passages suffices to show that if we are to speak of Jesus' experiencing God, we must speak also of his experiencing demons.

Jesus does not speak to the demoniac in the synagogue: he speaks to the demon in the demoniac. 'Be muzzled, and come out of him!' With the demoniac in the tombs it is the same: Jesus addresses the demon, 'Come out, the unclean spirit, out of the man', and he proceeds to ask the demon its name, so as to drive it out effectively. The reply is compound, '*My* name is Legion, for *we* are many', and the Legion then beg Jesus to be despatched into the pigs: 'and he commanded *them*'. At the foot of the mountain Jesus again speaks not to the boy but to the dumb spirit, 'Come out of him, and enter him no more': experience was all too common of demons that returned after a while with seven companions. 'No one,' says Jesus, 'can enter a strong man's house and plunder his goods unless he first binds the strong man': his forty days in the desert had been an intense spiritual struggle in which he felt he had 'bound' Satan, with the result that his exorcisms were possible. Mark says, 'He rebuked the wind and said to the sea, Silence, be muzzled': the wind is a *pneuma*, a breath/spirit, which must be rebuked, and the sea is addressed in just the same exorcistic formula, 'Be muzzled', as the demoniac's spirit. Jesus says, 'I saw Satan fall as lightning from heaven': this is not a hypothesis, but a moment of vision. He says at the Last Supper, 'Simon, Simon, Satan demanded to have you (all) that he might sift you like wheat; but I prayed for you. . .' Jesus has been in spirit in the court of heaven, and there he has seen Satan requiring the same sort of licence as he had to test Job in the Old Testament: and Jesus has interceded to save his disciples.

Of course we cannot be sure that all these comments go back to Jesus himself, but it is likely that at least some do; and if they do not, they stem from the same circle as Jesus, and it is very improbable that his experiences were different from these, as understood by the evangelists. Nor can it be helpful to brush them aside, as is done by Professor Trevor Ling,[2] as being so small a feature of the Gospel, in contrast to contemporary apocalyptic, where they bulk large. Of course they do: for the gospel is about the good news of the coming of God's kingdom, and the demons are in retreat. The point at issue, which seems to me as clear as daylight, is that Jesus experienced demons as real beings underlying madness, storms, dumbness and moral failure in just the same way as he experienced God as underlying life's blessings. So we must either accept that Jesus' experience of the transcendent was compelling, for us as for him, and conclude not only that God exists, but that demons exist; or we must allow that experience in large measure grows out of our world-view and so is fallible. In that case we are not obliged to believe in demons, but then neither are we left with a cogent argument for the existence of God. What then are we to say of the impressive experiences from more modern times which John draws from William James and Timothy Beardsworth, and also from his own youth? These were an effective part of Chapter 2, because they strike a genuine note, and there was a wise admixture of workaday milk-cans and gas-lamps (and buses!) with the more romantic (and so suspect) mountain top. Are these then to be written off as hallucinations?

John does not think that God intervenes in human affairs, so the great moments of illumination which he is describing are not, in his view, the result of an initiative of God to bring them about. They are, like everything else in our world, natural occurrences, in this case psychological occurrences. We do not know precisely how such 'peak' experiences occur, but it is easy to make suggestions. For example, conversions may often be found to follow a period of struggle which has depressed the spirits, and the resolution may then suitably be symbolized in an effulgence of light. Psychologists have often been interested in conversion experiences. S. de Sanctis' *Religious Conversion* (London 1927) was an attempt to isolate various traits of character common to Paul,

57

Augustine, Luther and others, together with elements common to their experiences before such enlightenment. C. G. Jung, in his *Contributions to Analytical Psychology* (ET London 1945), makes some suggestions to account for Paul's 'psychogenetic blindness'. W. Sargant, to whose *Battle for the Mind* I referred in Chapter 1, develops a theory of transmarginal inhibition. More recently, cognitive dissonance has been invoked by L. Festinger and others, e.g. in *When Prophecy Fails* (Minneapolis 1956), and has been applied to the experience of the Old Testament prophets by R. P. Carroll, *When Prophecy Failed* (SCM Press 1979). So even if we do not have adequate theories for explaining the psychological upheavals which underlie conversions, or other 'peak' religious experiences, it is not doubted that they are suitable matter for study, or that complete psychological accounts could, in principle, be given for them.

Now in other fields (and with other theologians) such psychological explanations would do nothing to diminish the possibility that they were experiences of something real. We may discover that G. E. Moore came from a bourgeois background, or had certain psychological kinks, and that will tell us why *he* wrote the works on ethics that he did; but such discoveries cannot tell us anything about whether his ethical theories are sound or not. So John may not be disturbed by the availability of explanations for religious experience: he may claim that such explanations say nothing about the reality.

But it seems to me that psychology does damage John's case, because that rests upon experience only. It would not matter if we were arguing with Thomists and we showed St Thomas Aquinas to be very peculiar, because the issue would be, 'But do his arguments work?' John is not claiming that Thomas's, or any other arguments work: experience to him is all, and if that experience becomes liable to explanation, it is weakened critically. For now the psychology operates as an *alternative* explanation to the 'reality' explanation, as when a man might say he had seen a flying saucer and his friends ask, 'Had you been drinking?' Drugs, alcohol, even cheese; a fit, a nightmare, a Walter Mitty temperament; any of these may seem an adequate explanation of an out-of-the-ordinary 'experience', and we should think it curious to press the question of whether there was really a ghost there as well. Surely, then, the same would apply to John's account of religious experience? He has himself excluded a divine initiative, so by his definition there will be a psychological explanation, and it will be complete: so it seems irrational to go in quest of reality as an additional explanation.

A book like Beardsworth's *A Sense of Presence*, on which John draws, is a very double-edged weapon. A married woman writes:

> This posed so many problems, financial and otherwise, that I turned to God for a solution. I knelt on the floor. . . As I opened my eyes, I beheld, in cursive writing, on the back of that chair, 'Missouri, receive you.' (My prayerful question had been: 'Should we move to Missouri?'). I stared in disbelief, shook my head and moved my eyes to another sort of chair only to see the same message there. This happened a third time.[3]

Now John does not believe in particular initiatives of God in human affairs, so he is obliged to think this good woman mistaken. God was not guiding her to go to Missouri, because he does not do that sort of thing: so the cursive writing on the chairs was a figment of her imagination. So it appears that some religious experiences, even though compelling, and indeed twice repeated, are not to be trusted. But if it has to be broken to her that she only *thought* it was God, but it was actually a deep psychological desire for Missouri (or whatever), what confidence is left to the man in the railway carriage with the milk cans, that he has experienced God, and not a deep psychological desire?

Another married woman writes:

> Our dog Judy died suddenly. Two nights later I was woken up somehow, and this is difficult to describe. I seemed to slide out of myself and stand by the bed, looking forward and to the right. I saw a warm glow with the dog standing there looking up at someone. I could only see the dog, but felt conscious of someone. It appeared that the dog was told to look at me. She saw me and curled up in pleasure. . .[4]

Some theologians have been driven to the desperate expedient of admitting dogs into the after-life, but I don't think John is one of them. If not, what is to be said of an experience like this? One can say that the experience is an experience of the divine 'someone', and that this is precipitated by the loss of a loved pet. But quite apart from the feebleness of such a move, we have here an instance of an experience of which the central focus, the dog, is explained as arising from the percipient's mind, and not from reality. What about the warm glow, then, and the out-of-the-body experience? They are both associated with the dog, so one would be inclined to dismiss them too. But then Beardsworth records dozens of warm glows, and sixteen pages of out-of-the-body experiences, and this would seem to reflect on them. We could of course take a firm line with the woman, and tell her that anything with a dog in it is no good, and that she has been seeing things: but Beardsworth rightly sees that this would not be fair, and indeed would prejudice the whole enterprise.

The only other comment I would make on the collection is that quite often (and it is only rarely that one can make a judgment) the people reporting the experiences seem to be in a highly wrought state or actually to be emotional people. A number have been recently bereaved, or speak of 'emotional and mental upheaval',[5] depression, etc. Sometimes one suspects that the percipient is a rather excitable person, like the lady who said: 'I was exceedingly anxious and self-reproachful over this matter of improper feeding of the infant, which had been due to the fact that immediately after his birth I had experienced the strange phenomenon of falling in love at first sight with a complete stranger who happened to be a visitor in my house.'[6] While I feel the propriety of John's warning that those of us who have not had moments of ecstasy should keep an open mind, it is not reassuring to learn that one such experience happened soon after childbirth to a woman ravaged with guilt and liable to fall in love with complete strangers. The percipients who provide the material for the book were self-selected: much the biggest number responded to advertisements in the newspapers. I cannot resist the suspicion that I – and all parish clergymen – have met such people: genuine, charming, pious, slightly off-beam. I should be very reluctant to take the great plunge of faith on the strength of their testimony.

There is one final consideration which seems to me to render John's case unconvincing, and that is the limited number of people who would claim to have had any experience of the kind he is speaking of. Firm figures are not available, and in any case depend on definitions. A Welsh GP in *A Sense of Presence* estimated that forty-five per cent of his patients had had experiences of their partners after being widowed. Claims of up to sixty per cent are somewhat surprisingly made, on limited samples, for experiences of the transcendent in general. I am not concerned to establish a figure, but only to observe that a very large number of people, including church people, do not claim to have experience of this kind.

This is true of clergy just as much as laity. I have frequently taught classes of clergy in recent years in which the topic of experience has come up, and I have often been impressed with the honest way in which some of the finest clergy have admitted to never having had a religious experience. I remember a Catholic priest saying, 'No, I've never had what I would call an experience of God'; and a Lutheran pastor said to me, 'Other people talk about experiences, but it does not generally boil down to much.' Bishop Robinson speaks in *Honest to God* about the emptiness of his prayer life at Westcott House, and his amazement when he discovered that others were in the same boat as he was.

I took part in a disquieting incident some years ago. I was put on a church appointing committee, and we interviewed four candidates for a quite important job. I was the last person to ask questions, and I felt that the others gave the candidates too easy a ride. As the university representative, I felt that I should try to find out if they had any stuffing in them. It seemed too offensive to say, 'Why do you believe in God, Mr Jones?', so I asked them, 'If you had to convince someone of why one should believe in God, Mr Jones, what would you say?' I was dismayed at the ease with which I could push them into a corner, unable to say anything simple, like, 'Well, if you pray, if you're anything like me, you'll find God is just there': but I was even more dismayed to find the committee equally flabbergasted. One canon said to me as we left the room, 'Well, I hope you're not on the committee when I apply for a job!'

Religious experience is, it seems to me, quite a rare feature of life for clergy and laity alike. Some have never had it; few claim to have it often. I have heard a man say, 'My prayers are the best part of the day for me', but after thirty years in the ministry I am obliged to say that I could count such remarks on the fingers of one hand. People do not say to one another in the church hall after the service, 'I find Christ's presence intensely near at the eucharist: wasn't it marvellous this morning?': and I do not myself think that

61

this is due to English reserve. It is very rare to hear a sermon on prayer that sounds convincing – or indeed to read an article on or a book about God at all that carries conviction. It is all these cases of the *absence* of the note which John says is so central which must strike a chill into the heart of the driven-snow Christian.

Now the point at issue is this. In John's theology our salvation lies in our knowledge of God. This world is a 'vale of soul-making' in which we know God at a distance, and it is a kind of primary school leading on to further worlds in which we will come to a fuller knowledge of him. In this John is only filling out the mainline insistence of the church that we are saved by faith, and see through a glass darkly: then we shall know even as we have been known. But it seems to be a corollary of this position that God should be making himself known without too much obstruction to the open-hearted man. The hard-hearted man of course cannot know him, because he has turned away. But we should have expected the open-hearted man to find it in some way *obvious* that God is there (at least intermittently) if experience of God is our only avenue to him. But this is exactly what we do not find to be the case. If I may put it in the form of an analogy: when I am old and bedridden, I may no longer write letters to my children, but wish very much to be visited by them. One of them may be hard-hearted: 'It's no good visiting the old man: he's become a cabbage.' But affection and duty may bring the others to my bedside. Now I may feel, like John's God, that it would not be good for them to be too overwhelming in warmth: I might be over-influential in their lives, or they might come hoping for a codicil in the will. But surely if I lay there year after year, and never moved a muscle for some of them, they would be justified in wondering whether their hard-hearted sibling was not right? Is not this, though, what we see in the church? If I were God, I'd let them see a twinkle in my eye sometimes.

To sum up, then, John's thesis seems implausible at a number of points:

1. It depends on the general reliability of our experience. But we think it irrational in normal life to trust experiences for which there is no public, outward and visible evidence; and such evidence is lacking in experiences of God.

2. It was indeed rational for Jesus, and saints of earlier ages, to

trust their experience of God to be veridical. But that experience was supported by a large web of public evidence, none of which John believes to be valid. It is irrational to accept Jesus' experience while disallowing the evidence undergirding it.

3. Even if we held religious experience to be *sui generis*, and sufficiently compelling that it would be irrational to distrust it, we still have the contradiction that Jesus experienced demons as well as God. One cannot at the same time say that Jesus' experience of the transcendent was so compelling that we should trust it, and that in a major area it was mistaken.

4. John allows that modern experiences of God have complete psychological explanations. But these must then function as competing alternative explanations of the phenomena; and in a number of particular reports John would himself wish to say that at least part of the experience was unconnected with a transcendent reality. The question must arise then how one can trust an experience to be of God.

5. Experience of God seems to be limited: some Christians have never had it, and few have it often. This seems to contradict a theology in which salvation is by knowledge of God, when open-hearted men seek a felt presence of God in years of prayer, and are disappointed.

4 Prayer, Providence and Miracle
John Hick

Let me first comment briefly on what Michael has said. For the most part he has been emphasizing that our experience, considered as cognitive, is fallible. It is possible for the soldier serving overseas to imagine that his wife has remained faithful to him when in fact she has not; for people to imagine mistakenly that someone returns their affection; for a person to feel grateful to a purely imaginary benefactor; and so on. All this is true enough. Indeed I made the same point myself, and Michael has added a series of vivid illustrations. But my own argument was not that every apparently cognitive experience is veridical and that therefore every religious experience is veridical. On the contrary, I was arguing that religious experience must, like other aspects of our cognitive experience, involve elements of human interpretation and projection; so that its full range includes not only the awareness of God reported by the great saints but also, for example, the delusions of religious fanatics who are convinced that God is calling them to slaughter their fellows. However, taking the saints rather than the fanatics as normative, I argued that those of us who participate, however faintly and peripherally, in the same broad field of religious experience are fully entitled to take the risk of trusting it as genuinely cognitive, and of living and believing on the basis of it. I do not think that this argument is overturned by the fact that there are such things as delusions, and that these occur in the religious as well as the non-religious realms.

Nor do I think that it is overturned by the fact, which I also acknowledged, that the great religious figures of the past, including Jesus, held a number of beliefs which we today reject as arising from the now outmoded science of their day, and that these beliefs must have affected the ways in which they experienced their environment. Thus Jesus, together with his contemporaries, believed that certain diseases (perhaps, for example, epilepsy) were cases of demon possession; and he doubtless experienced the dramatic energy of the epileptic syndrome as an invasive alien activity, and the divine healing power which flowed through him as driving out the demons. He also, together with his contemporaries, presumably believed that the sun circles round the earth and experienced this in the visible movement of the sun across the sky. Advances in medicine and astronomy have led us to think that he and his contemporaries were mistaken at these points. But it would not be reasonable to conclude from this that Jesus' experience of the reality and presence of God was a delusion. For the two matters are independent – as is shown by the fact that there are very many people today, sharing our up-to-date scientific understanding of medicine and astronomy, who also share in varying degrees in the religious experience of existing in the unseen presence of God. It is (as I have said before) theoretically possible that Jesus' experience, and indeed that *all* religious experience, is delusory; and it is equally possible that it represents the effect in human consciousnesses, at different times and in different circumstances, of the pressure of the divine presence upon us. But the fact that people have been mistaken in their scientific beliefs (as inevitably we also today will turn out to be in many respects), and therefore in the ways in which they have experienced the world, does not show that they were mistaken in believing that God is present to them.

Nor, again, do I agree with Michael that if Jesus had been asked why he believed in the reality of God he would have been likely to reply by citing what Michael calls the evidences of miracles, of divine interventions in Hebrew history, and of the orderliness of nature. He did of course accept, with his contemporaries, the world-view of first-century Judaism. But surely his uniqueness did not lie in this, but in his being so startlingly open to God, and his awareness of the demanding and re-creating love of the heavenly Father so powerful and luminous. It is because of this that what we sometimes refer to as 'the Christ event' constituted a new revelation, launching a new stream of religious experience which has been able to continue for nineteen centuries and to embrace hundreds of millions of people. The originating impulse of Christianity lay in Jesus' filial experience of God and in the life that expressed this, including his acts of healing, his teachings about the reality and love and claim of God, and his self-giving to the point of death; and in the new life, reconciled to God, which this engendered in his followers.

Again, Michael thinks that the fact that psychology can study the human conditions of religious experience, conversions, visions, etc. tells against the possibility that these experiences are the results of genuine contact with a transcendent divine reality. But that this does not follow was, I think, amply shown by William James in his classic discussion of the matter in *The Varieties of Religious Experience*. If God does not force the awareness of himself upon us, but is nevertheless always present and always gently pressing upon us, seeking our free response, psychology will be able to study the patterns of such responses, the conditions under which they tend to occur, and the environmental factors which tend to influence the forms that they take. For example, in late adolescence the hitherto somewhat amorphous personality often forms, either suddenly or over a period of a year or two, into a certain shape, with a certain shape of values. If the young person is sufficiently open to God this 'jelling' may take the form of a religious centring or even of a dramatic religious conversion. But the fact that we can observe that such centring is liable to occur at this particular stage of life does not, even in the slightest degree, constitute evidence against the authenticity of the new consciousness of God.

I would therefore reply to Michael's five points (on pp. 62f.) as follows:

1. The principle holds that it is rational to trust our apparently cognitive experience except when we have reason to doubt it. Is it then a 'reason to doubt' that God does not compel our awareness of him, as does the material world? Not on the theology which I advocate. For whilst our essential freedom as persons is not undermined by the coercive presence of the value-neutral physical environment, it would be undermined by the coercive presence of God as the ultimate reality in which being and value are one. There is no space to expound here this concept of our cognitive freedom in relation to God; but I have written about it at length elsewhere.[1]

2. I am glad that Michael recognizes that it was rational for the saints of earlier ages to trust their experience of God to be veridical.

I believe that their central and sufficient reason for believing in the reality of God was that they knew him in their own experience. The same is true of saints, and in lesser degrees of ordinary believers, today.

3. That Jesus experienced certain diseases as cases of demonic possession does not invalidate his experience of God. There are innumerable people who have, in lesser degree, shared his experience of living in the presence of God without sharing his first-century perception of disease. The two issues are independent.

4. There are also interesting psychological studies of disbelief and of atheistic conversion, which likewise suggest certain patterns.[2] Psychology, used polemically, is a double-edged sword; but in the end it is not really profoundly relevant either way.

5. The sense of the presence of God is indeed sporadic, and not experienced by everyone – not, for example, by Michael. For there is a necessary human element within the total event of our conscious encounter with God. It may even be that the kind of theology of divine interferences which he and many others have held inhibits rather than enables it, by leading people to expect miraculous divine interventions.

But when all these points have been made we are both – as I take it – agreed that the universe of which we are part is religiously ambiguous. It follows from this that it is possible – at least at this present stage of our existence – to interpret any aspect of it, including our religious experience, in non-religious as well as in religious ways. I am therefore not denying Michael's oft-repeated and lavishly illustrated point that such apparently cognitive experience is not infallible and that it *may*, in particular instances or in general, be delusory. By the same token, it *may* be an effect within human consciousness of God's non-coercive presence to us. And my argument has been that in this situation of theoretic ambiguity those who actually participate in this field of religious experience are fully entitled, as sane and rational persons, to take the risk of trusting their own experience together with that of their tradition, and of proceeding to live and to believe on the basis of it, rather than taking the alternative risk of distrusting it and so – for the time being at least – turning their backs on God.

In general it seems to me that Michael is reacting, very understandably, against the old and now largely abandoned form of

Christian apologetic, so popular in the eighteenth and nineteenth centuries, centring upon miracles, providential history, fulfilled prophecies and the apparently designed order of nature. That kind of apologetic saw God as demonstrating his presence by performing miraculous interventions in both natural and human history. It was a theology of divine interferences and manipulations: God answers prayers by miraculous suspensions of the order of the world; good harvests express his approval and disasters his anger; he protects Christian groups and nations against their enemies; and so on. I for one sympathize fully with Michael's – and many other peoples' – rebellion against such a conception of God and of his relationship to us and to the world. John Robinson's *Honest to God* (1963) was the classic expression of an increasingly widespread modern rejection of that anthropomorphic image of God as too small, too tribal and much too unimaginative. Michael was attracted – in company, paradoxically, with the fundamentalists – by its concrete, 'red-blooded' character. He has now been led, however, by theological criticism to reject it. His mistake, in my view, is not in rejecting it but in thinking that there is no other and more viable form of Christian faith.

Let us, then, turn to some of the central themes of red-blooded fundamentalist theology – prayer, providence and miracle – and look at them from a different Christian point of view.

We may begin with the idea of miracle. This can be defined in purely religious terms or in mixed religious and scientific terms. The purely religious concept denotes events which are experienced as having powerful religious meaning, events through which individuals or communities are vividly conscious of God, and which express to them the divine goodness or love or judgment. But when miracle is defined as a mixed religious and scientific concept the proviso is added that the events in question must be contra-natural, in the sense of being incapable of natural explanation. A miracle is then regarded as an event which could not have happened unless God, in his omnipotence, had intervened in the process of the universe to cause it to happen.

This latter is the traditional Christian concept of miracle, operating almost universally within Christendom until within the last hundred and fifty years or so. As Thomas Aquinas put it, 'those things must properly be called miraculous which are done by divine power beyond the order commonly observed in things'.[3] Or as David Hume, using essentially the same definition, said, a miracle is 'a transgression of a law of nature by a particular volition of the Deity'.[4] Various distinctions have been drawn (for example, by Thomas Aquinas) within the class of the miraculous conceived in this way; but let us concentrate upon the great historical miracles of the Bible, which were presented by the eighteenth-century apologetic as such important evidences of the existence of God.

There are legitimate points of view from which one can, in studying the biblical narratives, leave aside all questions of historical evidence and probability. One might, for example, see the stories simply as literary entities, and be interested perhaps in their structural similarities and dissimilarities as compared with other kinds of traditional narrative. But if our concern is to get at the truth concerning the events of human history then we cannot set critical questions aside. And when we embark upon historical criticism it soon becomes attractive to see these miracle stories as the recalling (usually in greatly exaggerated form) of memories of natural events which were experienced at the time as divine interventions. One of the most striking examples occurs in the Book of Joshua. There was a battle in which the Israelites triumphantly defeated the Amorites. The Amorites were for some reason demoralized before the battle, and the narrative gives as the reason that 'the Lord threw them into a panic before Israel, who slew them with great slaughter' (Josh. 10.10). As the Amorites were fleeing, large hailstones fell on them; and the narrative says, 'The Lord threw down great stones from heaven upon them . . . there were more who died because of the hailstones than the men of Israel killed with the sword' (10.11). And then finally, to complete their utter destruction, there was a long clear evening for the slaughter, so that with considerable poetic licence the Israelite bards could later sing that the sun stood still at Joshua's command whilst the Lord's enemies were wiped off the face of the earth. We may surmise that as the contagious faith of Joshua swept through their ranks, the people of Israel really did experience the hailstorm as a divine intervention on their behalf, and that later generations really did repeat believingly that the sun had stood still at Joshua's command to allow the massacre to be completed. For an imaginative reconstruction of the genesis of a comparable miracle story, read Richard Adams' gripping novel *Shardik*. The great bear, who is believed to be Shardik the incarnate Power of God, breaks loose amidst a battle and so terrifies the enemy, who see in it God fighting against them, and so encourages the Ortelgans, who are rising against their oppressors, that they smash through the demoralized army, capture the city of Bekla and overthrow an empire.

I am not going to set out to apply this kind of historical interpretation to the innumerable stories in the Bible of miraculous divine interventions in human affairs. This has been done often enough by those better qualified to do it. Let me instead simply acknowledge that such a treatment of the biblical material is possible and has indeed, to our twentieth-century minds, a certain inevitability. Further, the image of God as an occasional miracle-worker has lost religious plausibility for many today. The difficulty is one of consistency. For if it is consistent with God's relationship to his creatures that he should over-ride the structure of their world whenever he chooses, to reveal himself to them, to give them guidance, to answer their prayers, to save them from sickness and danger, why does he not do this more often and on a larger scale? Prayers rise every Sunday from thousands of Christian churches asking God to bestow peace, prosperity and justice on earth, to reconcile the nations and races, to impart wisdom to the world's rulers, to heal the sick, save the refugees, comfort the afflicted. . . These prayers remain very largely unanswered. Is God, then, unwilling or is he unable to put right humanity's multifarious wrongs and heal his multitudinous ills? Surely it is a more viable kind of theology which holds that God preserves and respects our limited freedom and responsibility by not making miraculous interventions that would over-ride the structure of our human environment. Such a theology renders the actual character of the world intelligible from the theistic point of view. But one cannot combine it with a belief in occasional miraculous interventions. To affirm these latter is to hold that they are consistent with God's way of dealing with his creatures; and then the inevitable question arises as to why God does not intervene more often and to better effect. Answers to this question generally appeal to mystery: we cannot know God's reasons for sometimes acting and more often refraining from acting. But this begs the question by assuming the point at issue, namely that God *does* sometimes act and sometimes refrain from acting. The more intelligible alternative is that God does not make miraculous interventions, in the sense of divine suspensions of natural law.

However, to set aside the idea of special divine suspensions of the divinely appointed structure of the world is not thereby to set aside all the reports of what have been called miracles. For the world is not a totally determined system within which every event, large and small, is mechanically necessitated by the previous states of the world. It is a partially open system within which the limited freedom of mental life is able to interact with matter and affect the developing pattern of events. The nature of mind and of its interactions with matter is perhaps the greatest mystery on the frontiers of science today, and it is at present only possible to speak in very general terms about the system of mental and psycho-physical law in virtue of which 'miracles' of healing, astonishing 'answers to prayer', remarkable instances of 'luck' and what Jung called 'synchronistic' events occur. But the time has long since arrived when we have to take serious account of the modern study of parapsychology. It seems overwhelmingly probable, for exam-ple, that human minds do at least sometimes influence one another directly in the way which we label 'telepathy'; probable that there is sometimes the awareness of events at a distance which is labelled 'clairvoyance'; and possible that there is the kind of physical action at a distance which is labelled 'psychokinesis'. Consider the bearing of all this upon 'miraculous' healings. When we add the probability of telepathy to the recent explosion of medical know-ledge concerning psychosomatic interactions, we have a possible general explanation of cases of bodily and mental healing, both with the laying on of hands and at a distance. The hypothesis which suggests itself is that when A heals B, A's mind influences B's mind telepathically at an unconscious level, and B's mind, again at an unconscious level, effects the physical processes of repair, perhaps speeding up and reinforcing these so that healing occurs much more quickly than it otherwise would have done, or even so that healing occurs in cases which otherwise would have proved fatal. When this is sufficiently sudden or unexpected it suggests divine intervention and has traditionally been called a miracle. But it seems an entirely reasonable, and indeed I would think probable, hypothesis that the divinely created laws of the biosphere are such that we do influence one another, probably to some extent all the time, through a continual telepathic interaction,

71

by the nature and quality of our intellectual and emotional activity; and that healings by prayer are dramatic instances of this. Within the awareness of God as both personal and purposive, healing through the influence of the mind upon the body is part of the universal divine action of creation/salvation. Indeed all healing, both physical and mental, and whether brought about by means of the laws known at a given time to orthodox medicine or of further laws beyond the present scope of medical knowledge, is God's work, in that healing is an aspect of the process by creation/salvation. The end-state being created by God's universal action through time can be described as a state of perfect health or wholeness in the fulfilment of the potentialities of human existence. But just because health, realized so far as our own individual and social patterns of life permit it, is an aspect of God's universal action, it would be redundant to postulate particular *ad hoc* divine interventions. To heal, both normally and 'miraculously', is to co-operate with God's prevenient activity.

However, in order to understand divine action in this way we require a theology according to which the whole process of the universe (and not only a few exceptional incidents within it) constitutes the divine creative action. Such a theological framework or hypothesis first began to be adumbrated, so far as Christianity is concerned, by Irenaeus and other of the early Greek-speaking Fathers of the church, and has since been developed further by Schleiermacher and many other more recent thinkers. This stands in contrast at many points to the Augustinian kind of theology which constituted Christian orthodoxy for some fifteen hundred years. A modern form of Irenaean theology would begin by recognizing that the universe is in incessant process through time and that this univeral process exists by God's will and for God's purpose. In so far as the divine purpose concerns and is known to mankind it is the purpose of creating perfected finite spiritual life; and we human beings are, or are part of, this life in the making. Our world is structured for the fulfilment of a phase of this purpose. As we see the divine purpose unfolding on earth, its first stage has brought man into existence through the long slow evolution of the forms of life; and the second stage, in the midst of which we are living, moves towards our eventual individual and corporate acceptance of the God-given potentialities of our nature. In the terminology of Irenaeus, man is developing through his own free interactions within the world from the 'image' to the 'likeness' of God. This is a process of growth through response to challenge from a state of spiritual immaturity to one of full humanity. And that the world, as an environment designed for this process, is basically good does not mean that it is free from pain and suffering, but rather (as Schleiermacher suggested) that it is suited for the fulfilment of the person-making process for which it exists. This divine purpose for humanity is manifestly not, however, normally fulfilled in this world, and we must presume that in God's creative purpose we continue to be held in being in other environments, probably constituting other spatio-temporal systems, within which further personal growth takes place.

On this understanding of creation as a continuous process there is no foundation for the traditional distinction between creation as an initial act at the beginning of time, and salvation as a later act designed to reverse the damage caused by our first forefathers' fall from grace. On the Irenaean view, creation and redemption form one complex event. However, since Christian language has so long been dominated by the polarity of creation and salvation, it seems advisable today, instead of abandoning the latter term, to conflate the two words into the hybrid 'creation/salvation'.

The whole process, comprising the evolution of the physical universe, the emergence of intelligent life and its development towards the end-state of perfected existence, is God's creative act. The entire process of the universe is the unitary divine action; and to be conscious of God is to be conscious of being part of his creative work and an object of his love. This form of religious experience is thus a consciousness of God as personal agent acting towards oneself and towards the whole creation. It is a conscious-ness of living in the presence of the divine Thou by whom one is intended, loved and upheld, and by whom one believes that one is being guided towards the fullness of eternal life.

Given this theological picture, can we properly speak of God *acting* towards us? The most basic and general conception of an action, as we use the word in relation to humanity and as we may apply it analogously in relation to deity, is that of an event enacting an agent's intention. In this basic sense God's continuous creation/salvation of the world is his action. For the existence of the world process, and within it the gradual creation through time of 'children of God', is the expression or enactment of God's intention. This divine action differs radically, however, from a human action in that it is coterminous with and as complex as the entire history of the universe. It is God's willing of a cosmic process within which finite persons are brought through their own free responses to an eventual perfection within the cosmic community of life.

The difference, then, between human action and divine action is that a human being is part of the world, acting as one part upon other parts, whereas God is the transcendent holy will enacting the entire world process – but enacting it so as to preserve our own finite freedom and responsibility within it. But God's continuous act of creation/redemption is a real action, a real expression or enactment of the divine intention. Its universality does not negate its character as personal action. The fact that God is acting simultaneously towards all his creatures and not only towards me, and that he is acting all the time and not only spasmodically, does not mean that he is *not* acting towards me. It means, rather, that God's action is of infinitely greater complexity and scope than mine.

To say that the entire process of the universe is God's action is not, of course, to say that God directly does everything that happens. That would be a doctrine of universal divine determinism. God creates us partly through our own freedom. Thus by no means everything that happens in this world is what God wishes to happen – except in the ultimate sense that he wills to exist a developing universe within which we were to emerge and be able to exercise our freedom. This has involved that the universe has an objective structure within which continuous change occurs in accordance with dependable regularities, with which structure and laws the creator does not interfere.

Is such a view adequate to the experience of divine activity in revelation, guidance and answer to prayer? I think that it is. Let us take first the experience of God's activity in self-revelation. I am speaking here primarily of the kind of religious conversion in which one experiences a powerful in-breaking from beyond one's own small self-centred world, the in-breaking of that which is limitlessly greater than oneself in being and in value. There is a powerful sense of the initiative and pressure of a reality beyond oneself. Very many people have experienced this, including myself as an eighteen-year-old student of Law, in a conversion to evangelical Christian faith. During a period of several days of intense intellectual and emotional ferment I was vividly conscious of a higher reality and truth pressing in upon me and seeking my recognition; and I was conscious of this at first as a deeply disturbing and unwelcome intrusion. And yet this pressure was not a force compelling me, but a truth or reality claiming my free response. And the outcome was that the world of Christian ideas and experience which had previously seemed incredible and unattractive became, as I took the step of commitment to Jesus as Lord and Saviour, the world in which I now lived with full assurance and joy in believing. I refer to this experience of my own, more than forty years ago, not as one that was in any way special, but on the contrary because it was in its main features a typical conversion experience such as many people undergo each year, often at the stage of life at which I was. And the question that I am raising is whether this kind of experience can be adequately understood without postulating a special divine volition in relation to each individual at the time of their conversion, a volition which God does not make in relation to other individuals or to that individual prior to that time. I do not think that any such miraculous interpretation of the conversion experience is called for; and indeed I think that such an interpretation would create serious problems of its own. For if God converts someone whenever he chooses to do so by causing that individual to have an experience such as I have described, then the question inevitably arises why he has not long since converted all mankind. If God makes his presence felt in this kind of way, whether we are ready for it or not, why does he make it felt by some and not by others? From the premise that conversion involves a special divine volition towards that particular individual at that particular time, there is a natural route to morally and theologically repugnant doctrines of double predestination such as we find in the thought of Calvin and many of his followers. But we do not need to adopt the premise from which such conclusions follow. We do not need to assume that conversion involves an arbitrary divine act. The alternative possibility is that God is continuously acting creatively and redemptively towards us and that a conversion represents a conscious human response at the time when, in his or her own growth and development, the individual is able to make it. These responses are probably normally 'threshold experiences', secretly prepared in the psychic life of the individual in a possibly lengthy process of inner change which at a certain point causes a transformation of consciousness in which one comes, relatively suddenly, to see all things in a new light. The form which the experience takes – whether it be evangelical Protestant, as in my own case, or Catholic or Orthodox or Pentecostalist, or indeed whether it occurs within a religious tradition other than Christianity – must, it seems obvious, depend very largely upon the religious influences amidst which the individual lives; and as the theistic explanation of the fact of conversion throughout the world it seems proper to postulate a continuous and universal divine creative/redemptive activity within which men and women come to an awareness of and response to God in their own cultural and personal circumstances. Religious conversion may, then, perfectly well be a real encounter with the divine reality; but it represents a particular human response to a universal divine self-disclosure rather than a particular disclosure directed and limited to that individual. And the form that conversion takes depends upon the contingencies of human history within which, sometimes, people suddenly become transformingly conscious of the divine presence in which they have always existed. But to account for this we do not need to postulate a further divine activity in addition to the universal divine act of continuous creation/salvation.

What, however, of divine guidance given to individuals in situations of perplexity? Does not God make his will known to those who earnestly seek it amid the complexities, ambiguities and dilemmas of their lives? Undoubtedly, many have received what they have believed to be guidance and illumination from above. Such experiences are not uncommon, and I can offer my own example. In the Second World War I was a conscientious objector on Christian grounds to military service. It was a very difficult question whether to take the absolutist line of refusing any kind of alternative service or to volunteer for the army's medical corps or for some such organization as the Friends' Ambulance Unit. Initially I was strongly inclined to the absolutist position, but was nevertheless in deep uncertainty, and prayed during a period of weeks for guidance. One morning I woke up with all my doubts completely resolved and with an absolute certainty that I must take the route of alternative service. It was utterly clear to me that I could not stand aside from the war, although I must not engage in its violence and destructiveness. And so I joined the Friends' Ambulance Unit and served in it for the duration of the war. The leading which I received was as clear and as morally compelling as if I had heard a voice from heaven. And the question is whether such experiences of sudden and decisive illumination in relation to a practical problem, when one has prayed for guidance, require us to postulate a particular divine operation upon the individual's mind, producing an effect in consciousness which would not otherwise have come about. I do not think that we are required to postulate *ad hoc* divine activity of this kind. The alternative view is that the illumination received is God's guidance by virtue of his universal action of creation/salvation. For it is part of his creative work that we are moral beings who sometimes wrestle with ethical dilemmas, seeking desperately to know what to do, and who pray to him for guidance and illumination. And when the illumination comes it is indeed the answer to our prayer. God has shown us the way, not by a psychological miracle but through our own intense desire for light and our readiness to follow it. With this powerful motivation we work out our doubts and perplexities until at last we arrive at a morally lucid awareness of our duty. Such illumination is not less truly divine guidance because it comes through the moral nature which God has given us within his continuous creative action. Once again, then, I do not think that we need postulate special adjustments to the universal divine activity; for as part of that activity God is already giving guidance to those who earnestly seek and are ready to receive it.

Very often, then, the answer to prayer – when it is prayer for guidance or for moral or spiritual help – is a change in ourselves. 'He who rises from his knees a better man, his prayer is answered.'[5] But what about prayers for changes in the world: for escape from danger, for bodily healing, for material prosperity, for victory in war. . . ?

Here, I think, we have to discriminate. Let us first set aside a wrong form of petitionary prayer. There are those who think it right to pray for divine interventions in the course of events, as the favours of a loving God to those who enjoy a special relationship with him as disciples of his Son. They will pray for sunshine or for rain, that a train will arrive on time, that they will pass an examination, or be offered a job, or be given a rise in salary, or win a war. The basic religious objection to such prayer is that it treats God as a tribal or family deity, or as 'my god', who will serve my interests or the interests of my group, if necessary at the expense of others. I was once returning by air from Washington to London and various arrangements depended upon my arriving fairly closely on time. However, the plane was delayed and took off some three hours late. If I had believed that God is ready to intervene on my behalf I might well have prayed for help with my journey. And if I had done so, on this occasion I would have found that my prayer was answered. For the usual westerly head wind across the Atlantic was so strong that night that the pilot announced at one point that we were flying faster than he had ever flown before, at almost the speed of sound; and as a result the plane landed at Heathrow on time. But if I had prayed for the exceptional journey that in fact occurred I should have been forgetting that the wind which speeded my own flight from west to east was to the same extent retarding flights from east to west, so that the convenience to myself and others flying in one direction must have been balanced by the inconvenience to the hundreds of passengers flying that night in the opposite direction.

I would suggest then that within a theistic mode of religious experience it is appropriate to be conscious of God's presence and activity in the beauties of the earth, in the happiness of human love and community, and also in significant events – healing, deliverances, new openings and opportunities – which seem to forward the development of ourselves or others towards whole-ness of being; but that we err, adopting inadequate theories which lead to further errors, if we hold that these providential happenings are caused by divine interventions in the course of the world. When our prayers for physical assistance or protection are 'an-swered' this is either due to our own or someone else's acting in accordance with psychic laws of which most of us know little or nothing; or simply to a fortunate coincidence – as in the case of the exceptionally strong wind which speeded my flight across the Atlantic.

According to the kind of theology which I am recommending, the eschatological meaning of each moment is its character as a cross-section of a history which is leading to the divinely intended end. For this reason any moment, any situation, can be the context of human God-consciousness. But in fact it is normal for us to be conscious occasionally, rather than continuously, of the divine presence. And naturally the occasions are generally ones which *we* can see, or think that we can see, to be forwarding God's purposes. These are the events for which we thank God – the victories and triumphs, the rescues and escapes, the healings and illuminations. It is generally in such events, rather than in defeat, sickness, failure and disaster that most of us are liable to become vividly conscious of God's presence. And so we call these positive and welcome events, amidst which we have been conscious of the gracious divine presence, acts of God. If I am conscious of God's presence while some calamity is being averted, or whilst my wife or child begins to recover from a serious illness, or when the bomb dropped near my house turns out to be a dud, or when I am saved from impending bankruptcy by some unexpected turn of events, then I may well experience these events as divine acts of deliverance. In doing so I shall probably assume that these fortunate events would not have occurred if God had not intervened to bring them about. But according to our hypothesis this assumption, although natural, is mistaken. God has created a world to be the environment of the creation – or rather, of a phase of the creation – of 'children of God'. As such it is religiously ambiguous, a realm of contingencies structured not for our comfort but for our growth, and offering tasks and challenges as well as moments of delight and happiness. Such a world contains both good and evil, both triumph and tragedy, both joy and suffering. And it is its character as a whole, as an enigmatic mixture of good and evil, calling for mutual love and service between human beings, that answers to the divine purpose. It is accordingly a mistake, although a very natural one, to assume that the good moments come from God and the rest from somewhere else. The entire mysterious interweaving of light and shadow comes ultimately from God; and no one detail, in contradistinction from another, is directly arranged by God. The details constitute a realm of contingency whose inscrutable element of chance is essential to the character of the world as a sphere of person-making. But although we are deluded when we single out moments of deliverance and triumph as divine acts, this does not mean that that deliverance or triumph, through which we have become joyfully conscious of God, is *not* part of God's action. For it has occurred within God's act of creating and sustaining a person-making world, and it does express and embody his loving-kindness towards us. But our isolating of this particular bit of God's universal action expresses a limitation in our own religious awareness. Thus our experience of divine activity within a particular situation is authentic, even though our implicit denial of divine activity in the wider creative process is mistaken and is indeed contrary to a central Christian insight. For the capacity to find God in suffering and defeat as well as in triumph and joy is perhaps the special genius of Christianity. The power of the cross in Christian experience arises from its making visible the inescapable interplay of good and evil within the creative process. For Christianity declares that the sufferings of the righteous can work for the salvation of all. Even human malice and human pain can eventually be made to serve the divine purpose. Accordingly the saints are conscious that in the whole of life, in both its easy and its hard passages, we are having to do with God and God with us, and that life's ultimate meaning is that it leads to the kingdom of God.

This is the kind of understanding of God's presence and activity in the world that I would commend to Michael as consonant both with Christian experience and with the knowledge of the universe currently made available to us by the sciences.

5   The Action of God

Michael Goulder

Last September we witnessed a natural uncomfortableness. The Queen and the Prime Minister and the Cabinet and the leaders of the Services wished to attend St Paul's Cathedral for a Service of Thanksgiving in connection with the end of the Falklands War, and the Archbishop of Canterbury and the Dean wished them to come; but there was no agreement as to what was to be said in the service. I am not concerned here with the political differences, and the way in which Dr Runcie steered a middle path with his customary skill; but with a much more fundamental religious question. Whether you had come to thank God for our victory, like Mrs Thatcher, or for the courage and skill of our forces, or just for the whole shambles coming to an end fairly quickly, and without major loss of life and national honour, the fundamental religious question is the same: what sort of thing are we thanking God for doing? What sort of action do we take it that God performed, for which we are to thank him?

In Chapter 3 I made the distinction between red-blooded theologies and driven-snow theologies, but clearly there are shades of red. With an old-fashioned, crimson theology, there is belief in miracles. That is to say, to give an instance, one might think that an Exocet missile had been launched from an Argentine aircraft and was homing in on *HMS Invincible*; but at the crucial moment God deflected the electronic device so that it missed the carrier and fell harmlessly in the sea. Those with such a theology can certainly say 'Thank God'. It is worth while remembering that such beliefs were standard in the days of an earlier invincible Armada nearly four centuries back. The Spanish fleet sailed in expectation of a miracle, for they were sailing under papal blessing to regain an apostate province of the church. But the English fleet also sailed in expectation of God's action on their side. It was not yet understood that to pierce the oaken sides of men-o'-war it was necessary to close to very close range, and when one English captain had bombarded the enemy all day without effect, he said, 'It is for our sins' – in other words, God was preventing the cannon-balls from penetrating the hulls. When the Spanish fleet finally dispersed, Queen Elizabeth had medals struck with the legend, 'God blew with his winds and they were scattered.'

The God who thus prevents cannon-balls from taking effect, and blows Catholic ships on the rocks, is out-of-date, in the sense that probably most of those gathered in St Paul's Cathedral held a crimson theology of this kind. Brian Hanrahan, an eminently sane BBC reporter sheltering behind a gorse bush outside Goose Green, remarked amid the hail of machine-gun fire and the mortar bombs: 'In such conditions one comes to sympathize with the soldiers' common saying, "If it's got your name on it, you've had it." ' Put more theologically, what is implied is this. God has the final hand in the battle, and he decides who is going to be killed and who is not. No doubt he is a merciful God, and sees that most of the fire goes astray; but it is unreasonable to expect that every bullet will miss, and some he permits to go home. This seems a more friendly view of the divine love than to suppose that God literally directs some bullets to the heart; rather he directs all the other bullets to miss. Such crimson theologies are of course encouraged when series of Argentine bombs hit warships and fail to go off. Perhaps (people feel) the whole campaign was won because of the bombs which failed to detonate, and that is what we are thanking God for.

Crimson theologies are not as popular as they were, and you will not find them taught in the University of Birmingham; nor do I think that many of the clergy in St Paul's would have subscribed to them. We feel today that the whole notion of God intervening in this way is rather crude. We can see that the notion of God being on the Catholic or the Protestant side in 1588 was small-minded and parochial. We know that cannon-balls will only go through oak if they are fired from closer to, and that ships going round the north of Scotland in sixteenth-century winters, without adequate seamanship, were liable to shipwreck without God taking a hand. We also find it hard to explain why God should spare the *Invincible* but not the *Sheffield* or the *Atlantic Conveyor*, if he monkeys about with electronics. It makes him seem arbitrary or favouritizing. The so-common complaint of the bereaved, 'Why should this happen to me?' is a not unreasonable response to such a theology. The clergyman's defence, the inscrutable wisdom of God, is felt justly to be an evasion. What sort of a God is it who puts the names of young soldiers on the nails in an IRA bomb? And there is the further difficulty that much human endeavour is reduced to folly. We wonder at the selfless courage of the Argentine airmen who pressed their attacks home in San Carlos Bay in the face of suicidal losses; but God, on this theory, is quietly manipulating the bombs so that they will not go off even when they hit. So on many fronts the whole thing loses credibility: it is only necessary to expound it to see that we do not believe it.

Crimson theologies are not the only ones with red blood in them: people with hardened arteries may thin their blood (I suppose) to a deep pink, and without suggesting that the church has hardened arteries, one may note that you can still believe in a God who responds to this world's needs without the crudities I have outlined. People often say, 'I believe that God works through people', and although they might wish to retain an option on miracles – say in the New Testament – they would not wish to invoke them much in everyday life. Now the phrase 'God works through people' is ambiguous, for it may mean that God is beaming out good influence all the time, and he works (effectively) when people respond to it – that is John's position. But it may mean that God takes the initiative by influencing people's judgments and wills *so that they do things which they would not otherwise have done*: and that is the position which I am labelling deep pink. Thus people may give thanks for the courage and skill of the Forces, thinking that when it came to the crisis our men had just that extra endurance and toughness which the Argentines lacked, and that this was due to the grace of God. Major Christopher Keeble, who commanded the Second Battalion of the Paratroops after Colonel H. Jones was killed, attributed their victory in part (to the surprise of some) to their being religious. Or a letter appears in *the Times* saying that we are thanking God for the resolution of Mrs Thatcher and other leaders: again the assumption is that God provided grace to keep Mrs Thatcher to her decisions, a thing which she would not otherwise have been able to do. Otherwise there is nothing to thank him for.

Deep pink theologies are more appealing than the crimson varieties, and you will find at least one member of the Theology Department in this University who is deep pink; but they are faced with exactly the same objections, and their attraction is meretricious. For what is the difference between God interfering with the electronics of the Exocet, and his interfering with Mrs Thatcher's brain circuits? If, on the hypothesis, she was just about to cave in to the insistent pleas for 'negotiation' by Mr Foot and Señor Perez de Cueillar, and God deflected her judgment, then surely the intervention is just as crude. We still have a miracle on our hands, that is, an interference with the sequence of events that would otherwise have obtained; and it only seems less crude because we can see the Exocet being deflected and we can't see Mrs Thatcher being deflected. But psychological miracles are just as much miracles as mechanical miracles – indeed, with electronics, the scale is not much different.

So we have exactly the same two objections that we had before: the deep pink God is as arbitrary and as manipulative as the crimson one. What is the sense of thanking God for intervening and stopping Mrs Thatcher from weakly giving way in the crisis? Why didn't he intervene a bit earlier with General Galtieri's brain circuits and save the whole business, and thousands of lives? Or even 'inspire' Mrs Thatcher to see that the trouble was on the way? So God seems arbitrary, and the only defence is his 'inscrutable wisdom', which is another way of saying that we cannot make head or tail of it, but we are not going to give up our theology. But the manipulation objection is worse with the pink theology. We had given Mrs Thatcher credit for her resolution, and had decided to vote for her again next time, since she seems to have a bit more spunk than the others, and may do as much harm to Mr Scargill as she has to General Galtieri. But now it turns out that she was going to have given way to Senor de Cueillar, and God had to work a mini-miracle to bring us through. We can have no confidence in regular miracles and shall have to vote for the SDP. In other words, the God who works through people in effect takes away their freedom and their dignity. We cannot give any credit to people for their virtues with safety any more, for we are always liable to be told that it was God's inspiration, grace, and so on, that turned the scale. Where is the sense, then, of giving 'H' Jones a VC? On this theology he might have been only mildly courageous in himself, and it was God who made all the difference.

I have taken the Falklands as an illustration of the weakness of these two theologies, but what I have said surely applies to every department of life. For instance, Cardinal Hume holds a red-blooded theology, whether crimson or pink I cannot tell you – perhaps cardinal red. We must sympathize with him, because he made a very forgivable theological statement four years ago which turned out to be rather embarrassing. Returning from the election of Pope John Paul I, he said, 'We have elected God's candidate.' I am not privvy to the secrets of the Vatican election chamber, but the situation is easily imagined. Forty-five per cent of the cardinals, let us say, arrive determined to vote for Cardinal Conservativo of the Vatican Curia. Forty-four per cent have come to give their vote for Archbishop Liberale of Brazil. Prayer is said, and hearts are made open to the Holy Spirit; and it at once becomes clear that God's man is the charming, light-hearted Venetian, who is duly elected. But then, alas, the job kills him off in a month. Ah, the inscrutable will of God! How unsearchable are his judgments and his ways past tracing out! But even those who defend this position have trouble with the election of some of the earlier popes. What about the Borgias? If it is a bad election, we can always debit it to sin, and give the credit for a good election to God; but that does look like 'Heads I win, tails you lose.' And the 'God's candidate' theory also makes nonsense of the way in which normally responsible electors try to size up which candidate has the gifts for the present needs of the community. If you do that, you will end up with what *seems* to be the best candidate by *human* wisdom: better just pray to God to manipulate your mind to his choice, which you would not have discovered otherwise. For of course if you could have discovered it by your own judgment, then God has done nothing, and you have nothing to thank him for.

I do not know if I have persuaded any red-blooded readers of the unattractiveness of their arbitrary and manipulative God; but at least I hope that I have persuaded you to think more kindly of John. He is not a beast of deliberate unbelief at all: he is an honest man doing his best to salve what he can from the wreck, and his position is that of most academics, in fact, even though they may not like to be seen in the company of someone who puts things so clearly and bluntly. A Finnish friend of mine, an NT scholar, commented, 'The first virtue of a theologian is obscurity.' Better, John feels, to give up the whole idea of an intervening God altogether. It is a piece of theological naivete. God is there all the time beaming out his love and care. He has so set up the world that almost everyone has some chance of spiritual growth, which is what matters. As we respond to his loving influence, so we begin to experience the blessedness of relationship with him, which will be fulfilled hereafter. He never takes a particular initiative, so he is never arbitrary or manipulative. In the Bishop of Durham's epigram, 'He acts by being believed in.'

Before making some comments on John's driven-snow view of providence I should say a brief word about the possibility of any intervening position; for you will be very properly suspicious of any attempt to categorize all theologians as red, pink or white. What, you may feel, about the incarnation and the resurrection? They have not had much of a mention yet. So we should make reference to theologians like Emil Brunner[1] or John Lucas,[2] who have dispensed with the traditional doctrine of providence, that is, the full red-blooded theology, whether crimson or pink, but who retain belief in a limited number of intervening acts of God which include at least these two, and may extend as far as the call of Isaiah and St Paul – in other words enough to initiate the history of man's salvation. It is true that this view does not give you much to say about the Falklands, but it has the enormous advantage of retaining some link with orthodoxy and also giving some reason for believing in God.

Nonetheless, I cannot recommend it. When we were having the sitting-room painted some years ago, the decorator advised us to put a few drops of red in the white paint for the walls to make it more cheeful, and told us that the tint we have was called 'magnolia'. So Brunner's is a magnolia theology, and it suffers from the implausibility of magnolia views the world over. When I was young I was told, 'Science has explained almost everything, but it cannot explain how life began or how man received a soul.' That position is now justly resigned as a 'God-of-the-gaps' view. When we have explained so much, it looks likely that we shall soon explain the few remaining problems; and with mega-molecules and amino-acids and talking chimpanzees and skulls of homo this and homo that, there are not so many people talking these days about the 'gaps' which science cannot explain. With so few drops of red in the white paint, it looks as if we could dispense with them too; the colour may not be so cheerful, but it is more honest. And so it is with magnolia theologies. When so much else of God's traditional initiative is now withdrawn, one is bound to ask, 'Should we not look critically at the resurrection too?' After all, the only established facts are the conversion of Peter and the others, and their belief that Jesus was raised: is it not possible that Peter was just converted, and his conversion took the form of a vision? I will not discuss the incarnation, because that is a big subject, and John has put together, and our Editor has published, an excellent little book about it which has enjoyed a mild success, called *The Myth of God Incarnate*. I particularly commend the two chapters on the New Testament. One may also perhaps reflect on the implausibility of a theology which allows that the world has been going for four billion years and posits only two actions of God, one 1982 and one 1952 years ago; or half a dozen to a dozen more, clustered around the same period.

So one cannot but sympathize with the move John has made to withdraw God completely from the scene of initiatives and interventions. No God of the gaps for him, even the historical gaps; and he has sketched in for us with his customary force and clarity an outline of the field of God's action which results from this. It remains for me therefore in the second half of this chapter to consider the implications of his outline.

Perhaps the first thing to strike the reader accustomed to traditional Christianity is how little, in John's view, God does. He 'creates' the world, though not quite in the traditional sense of the word, and we must examine that in a moment; and he is present to his creation, influencing for good all who attend to his loving presence. Most of the props of the traditional Christian drama are gone: there is no original sin, no election of Israel as God's people, no incarnation, no resurrection, no providence, etc. If these words are to be used, they will be used in rather stretched senses. Suppose one were to ask if such a theology is altogether novel, the answer is (if I may return John's compliment) that it is rather an eighteenth-century theology. It is close to the view known as Deism, which retained belief in God as creator, but dispensed with original sin, the election of Israel, the divinity of Jesus, providence

87

and so on; the view whose most famous exponents were the French writers, Rousseau and Voltaire. John's theology has more to it than Rousseau's, but there is a marked family resemblance. The Savoy vicar in *Emile* (1762) believed in God, the soul and the future life, and grounded this faith in the sense of a relationship with God through the conscience – not too far from John's experience of enlightenment on the pacifist issue, which I found so striking.

I do not introduce Deism for the cheap purpose of blacking by association, but to warn the reader of the road ahead. Santayana said: 'Those who do not study the history of ideas are doomed to repeat it.' Rousseau is usually regarded as the forerunner of humanistic liberalism. He and other bold spirits saw the writing on the wall for traditional Christianity, and proposed a half-way house. But a century later, in the 1860s, the crisis came for such religious elements as the Deists had retained, with the arrival of positivist philosophy and the advance of science and of biblical criticism. Thereafter we see a double reaction. The Deists, and their associates the Unitarians, tend to lose strength and become atheists; and indeed the greater part of the people of Europe have tended to go the same way, in practice if not by confession. But the church was able to mount an impressive revival, in both the Catholic and Protestant churches. For a hundred years, from Pius IX's *Syllabus Errorum* in 1864 until the Second Vatican Council, the Catholic Church was able to turn its back quite effectively on modern thought; and so learned and sensitive a man as the Anglican Archbishop Ramsey could still write in the 1960s as if the traditional Christian doctrinal edifice were the Rock of Ages. But the tide has in fact been ebbing fast. Education, industrial work and other factors have estranged working people from the church in millions, and the revival is now able to maintain its momentum only in ghettos – socially isolated groups like fundamentalists or Pentecostals, or isolated societies with special social pressures like Ireland and Poland. To most people in the West, the kind of considerations that John and I have set out in the last chapter and a half make a red-blooded theology impossible. We are driving over the same course as our eighteenth-century forefathers, only at four times the speed.

John's clear eyes see that the red blood of traditional theology will not save the souls of men in the 1980s; and like the Deists before him, he is saving what he can from the wreck. But the deistic God was sacked in the nineteenth century for doing no work; and we may reasonably enquire how much work the God of John's theology does. The greater part of his chapter is to explain what God does *not* do. But then, if our prayers are answered by our resolutions to be a better man; if our conversions are the resolution of long-latent doubts, reached through honest wrestling by us; if marvellous healings are due to telepathic forces within us, still half-understood; and all the biblical miracles are exaggerated memories of deliverances misunderstood as divine interventions; then we are driven back to the question with which I began this essay, 'What sort of thing, then, does God do?'

The Deists felt they had their feet on firm ground over creation: it was obvious that the universe must have got started somehow, and it could hardly have started itself. The natural recourse was to take Genesis 1 as true in outline, but (increasingly) wrong in time-scale: God created the universe, only not in 4004 BC but, say, in 14,000,000,004 BC. Today it is not obvious that the universe 'got started': after all, space seems to go on for ever, so why should not time, and matter too? Present scientific opinion is that the universe we know all originated in one 'big bang', but no one knows if there was a 'before the big bang': perhaps, it is speculated, there has been a kind of concertina history of matter, with alternate explosions and implosions. In the present phase everything is moving away from everything else at increasing speeds; perhaps everything was rushing together in the previous phase, and it was this that caused the big bang. This is not the only possibility; but in an area where we have no knowledge, we have learned the wisdom of not being dogmatic.

There are thus two distinct questions in the modern mind, where there was only one for Rousseau. One is a question for the physicists, 'What is the history of the universe?' and to that John naturally wishes to return an agnostic answer. The other is a question for philosophers, 'Why should the universe exist?'; and to this he gives the positive answer, 'It exists because it is created by God; and God is eternal, and by definition requires no explanation.' John refers to this briefly in Chapter 2, and at slightly more length in Chapter 6, though he concedes that it in no way constitutes a proof of God's existence (as it did for the Deists). It gives theism the advantage, though, he argues, in so far as it is a more satisfactory explanation of the experience of the universe if it depends upon a self-existent creator than if it is brute fact. So here is the first work which the God of John's theology does; and as he speaks of 'the entire process of the universe' as 'the unitary divine act', we may say that it consists of God's creating and sustaining of the universe.

Bare creation, however, does not cover all that John requires, for he speaks of the world as 'an environment designed for' our maturing into full humanity. He says that 'the universe is in incessant process through time, and this universal process exists by God's will and for God's purpose': this process he calls 'creation/salvation'. The introduction of words like design and salvation take us beyond the naked notion of God's creatorhood: things do not merely hold their existence from him, but the whole process operates under his designing act. So, since we are agreeing to use the contemporary scientific view of the big bang as the starting point of the universe we know, we may get some sort of idea of the kind of thing God is thought of doing: put very crudely, he programmed the big bang. In speaking so, we may keep open the options I have just referred to. If the big bang were the absolute beginning of time and matter, then God created the universe by programming the big bang. If the concertina theory were correct, God could either have programmed the whole sequence to culminate in a designed big bang, or he could have taken a second specific action to produce the required effect; and so on. The point is that the essential make-up of our world, and all other worlds, was settled in those first few seconds: the limits of salinity of our water, the vital component of carbon, and many other things without which life, as we can imagine it, would be impossible. So the sort of thing that God did was so to programme the explosion that the heat was 10^x degrees rather than 10^y degrees. If matter were everlasting, it might be easier to think of this design-action as distinct from the creating sustaining action: but it would be more congenial to John if it were one act, a 'unitary divine act'.

Once this is done, John is adamant that God leaves his creation to develop in the direction in which he has set it: there are no interventions. The way in which it was set up has ensured that it gradually evolved into the world we now live in. God has always been present in his universe – however we may think of that presence – delighting or grieving over his handiwork. When, after so many billions of years, man arrives on the scene, God's presence is thought of as having secondary effects. Men and women are aware that he is there, and feel the call to respond to his will. This is at first understood ceremonially: he wills us to recognize him in worship. Later this extends to felt ethical demands, and we have the whole web of claimed religious experience which John described in Chapter 2. But even here it is important to remember the unitariness of the divine action. The personal, 'Missouri, receive you' type elements, are put in on our side. God is (to use an only slightly naughty comparison) like one of those American radio stations that broadcast the gospel twenty-four hours a day; all we have to do is switch it on. But God is concerned for each of us in our personal growth into his likeness: it is only that he never makes a personal initiative.

God's unitary act, then, has three aspects, and these are in a way distinct. The design aspect is limited to the past, whether to creation in the traditional sense, or to the moment of the big bang if the two do not coincide. The sustaining aspect is continuous through all time, and if matter is everlasting, then creation belongs here too. The 'broadcasting' aspect, whereby he makes his presence known and his will felt, is limited to the brief period in which mankind has arrived on the evolutionary scene. The impact of this third mode of divine action is not to be undervalued, for although experience of God in any sharp form may be rare among individuals, yet the cumulative effect upon mankind through the 'churches', the communities of the great (and lesser) religions, may be judged to be very considerable. These are the three modes of the divine action of creation/salvation in this world: of course, further action will have to be predicated for the worlds beyond in which we are to mature further into God's full likeness.

Universal belief-systems, such as are offered by different religions and non-religions, and by different thinkers within them, compete with one another on two levels. One is an intellectual level: they must seem *possible*, to win any adherents at all, and to be successful they must seem *plausible*, or likely to be true. The other is the emotional level: they must *satisfy* our needs – to feel cared for, forgiven, meaningful, etc. While it seems arrogant to me to suggest (as is often done) that ordinary people are concerned only with the emotional level, it is unrealistic to suppose that even intellectuals

91

weigh possibility and plausibility first, and then opt for the most satisfying of the remaining candidates. Theology is a difficult and abstract business, and implausibilities are easily overlooked when the deepest concerns of the heart are involved.

The attraction of John's theology is that it is clearly possible on the one side; and on the other it enables us to continue as members of the historic church, to maintain its central tenet, the existence of God, and to set our lives within a framework that is at once meaningful and hopeful. Its disadvantages are that it is not very plausible; and that it leaves much of man's emotional need unsatisfied. It is the first of these which is my main interest.

If it were established that nothing existed before the big bang, then there would be some apparent return from John's theology: it would be more satisfying to have a self-existent God as the ultimate explanation than a brute fact bang from nothing. But it is not at all clear that this return is real. First, the logical process looks very suspect. This world does not explain itself; therefore it derives its existence from a creator. But how do we explain the existence of the creator? Oh, his existence is self-explanatory. We are reminded of Thales saying that 'the earth is supported by water, on which it rides like a ship'; which was all right until someone asked what the water was supported by. Second, it is a complex question, and in doubt, whether the notion of God being self-explanatory is coherent.[3] John refers to this discussion in Chapter 6, and certainly the case against its coherence has not been made; but it cannot be assumed that the idea makes sense. Third, it would be very convenient if the universe were so ordered as to yield the most satisfying answers to our questions: but why should we suppose that this pleasing state of affairs obtains? That it does so in scientific matters (give or take the odd paradox) should not lead us to assume that it will necessarily be so in metaphysical questions also. Perhaps in the last resort there are just some brute facts.

With the programming of the big bang, John is up against the weakness of the magnolia theologies I referred to earlier. If *everything* since the first three minutes of the universe has proceeded according to natural processes discoverable in principle by scientists, then it seems more plausible to suppose that the events of those first three minutes were also due to natural processes preceding them, than to suppose a cause of a totally different kind.

A theological explanation is possible, but a natural explanation is more plausible. God is filling the last gap in the God-of-the-gaps-view, creation. But just as we have come to think differently about the soul, and about the origin of life, in our own lifetime, does it not look as if we may in time fill this last gap of all, and dispense with the creator as we have with the giver of souls?

Further, if matter is everlasting, it becomes obscure what the action is which is described by the word 'creator'. What did God actually do? If we say, 'The world just exists in his mind: he thought it up, as a novelist thinks up the plot and characters of his novel', then it would seem that the universe is only on a par with all the possible universes which may have occurred to the mind of God. We may say, 'How can we expect to answer this kind of mystery?': but then the plausibility of a theology depends to a fair extent on our answering the questions it evokes. It is competing with a naturalistic position in which they do not arise. There is no problem to a humanist about what action 'sustains' an everlasting universe in being: no action seems to be required.

John refers in Chapter 6 to a series of problems which we cannot discuss adequately here. The most important of these is the problem posed to his, as to all theologies, by the existence of so much suffering in the world. I do not intend to enter these lists here, but merely to agree with John that 'it constitutes the most formidable barrier that there is to such a belief'. Even with so weighty an apologia as John has himself written in *Evil and the God of Love*, the believer never quite escapes the doubt that his creed is involved in a major implausibility. Here again, the humanist alternative is not under threat, for there suffering is due not to God but to natural causes and to human ill-will or carelessness: our task is, as Marx said, not to explain the world but to change it.

There is, however, one particular problem which is raised by John's account. He says that the universe is designed by God for our maturing into his likeness: this world is 'a vale of soulmaking'. In other words, the process is *educational*. The changes and chances of our life here, the result of God's initial creative action, are to teach us to become true sons of God. In this point John differs from much traditional Christianity, in which man was just *saved* by grace. With traditional salvation, plausibility does not arise. We cannot tell by looking at a man if he has been justified by God or not. But with an educational model, plausibility does arise: we

93

are bound to ask ourselves, Does it look as if this is a well-run school or not? Do God's children look as if they are making progress, and will be ready to graduate?

John, of course, has seen this question coming, and has written at length about it in *Death and Eternal Life*: for it is obvious that most of us are neither black nor white at death, and the simple judgment-at-death, no-second-chance picture will not do for him. He therefore posits a series of 'worlds' for our growth into God's likeness, and the plausibility of these also must be left aside for now. But, if we restrict our attention to God's purposive action in this world, which John has set out in Chapter 4, we are still left with the plausibility question. Granted that this world is only, so to speak, a primary school, is it a well-run primary school? Are we making progress, and will we be ready to graduate?

It must raise a question about the school image when we reflect that probably half of all the children who have ever been born have died before the age of two. What are we to say about them? Do they just move on, and miss out on their whole primary school experience? But a more general problem seems to be the observable fact that people harden their attitudes as they grow older. When we are young, we may be brought to better ways of thinking: it is hard to change old people, who may be set in complacent, prejudiced and unrealistic ways. Now John justifies the existence of this 'ambiguous' world on the basis that we need freedom, and so some distance from God, in order to become ourselves, and grow in independence into his likeness. But what we seem to observe is a very partial progress in most people, coupled by a partial regress. If then God needs to withdraw much of this freedom and independence in the 'secondary school' ahead, in order to break down our set ways, why was it of such importance in the first place? But if exactly the same freedom is to be available there as here, I am not applying for the post of teacher of the remedial class in the next life; for I do not see how the pupils can learn.

So although John presents a possible theology, it seems to me to be beset by implausibilities. Even the plausibility of creation is not at all as clear as it was. The intrusion of a divine cause to programme the big bang, and so the history of the universe, into an otherwise natural sequence of causes, looks dubious. If, as is possible, matter is everlasting, the meaning of 'creation' is unclear. The picture of the world as a primary school does not seem coherent with the high death-rate of the very young, or the unteachability of the very old. There are further difficulties undiscussed over the problems of suffering, and of conceiving a likely progression from this world to the beyond. But above all, as I argued in Chapter 3, there is really no rational basis offered for accepting such a picture. After all, we have called the book *Why Believe in God?*

John aims to give an account of a religion, not just a framework of belief, for modern man; and for this purpose, as I have said, he needs to satisfy the emotions as well as the intellect. But I fear that not very many of the emotional satisfactions that were supplied by traditional Christianity are still met by his slimmed-down version.

The old red-blooded religion had a lot going for it. It carried the authority of heaven, which was more even than that of the University of Birmingham. It set our community, the church, in he centre of history, as the successor to God's people, Israel. Its wonders were impressively foretold by prophets in the Old Testament. It culminated in the supreme act of divine humility, the incarnation. It moved the heart by the word of God's compassion. It hushed man's guilt by the blood of the cross. It assured his adherence to Christ by the mystical union of baptism and the eucharist. It comforted his anguish with the confidence of providential action. A powerful and revered priesthood, rising to the Crown or the Tiara, directed his paths in doubtful ways, and was at hand when he died.

Of this impressive structure John retains the central figure, God, but in an austere and attenuated form, and at the cost of almost all his traditional action. John says that 'it is appropriate to be conscious of God's presence and activity in . . . significant events – healings, deliverances', etc: but his activity is so very remote, and not personal at all, that it is hard to feel that gratitude would be a proper feeling. The polio bacillus exists by God's creative will, just as much as the Salk vaccine; and the liver fluke and the malaria mosquito are the work of his hand. Earlier John writes: 'To say that the entire process of the universe is God's action is not of course to say that God does everything that happens': but the exceptions he then specifies are those of human action contrary to God's wish. Most of the deliverances for which the pious have felt moved to thank God are similarly, on John's account, no more his willed action than the disasters. If it is irrational to pray for a westerly wind (in John's instance), it is equally inappropriate to thank him for one.

It is not only God whom John retains, but, like Rousseau, the soul and eternal life; and it is here that he still gives us a motive for believing, for he provides our lives with a meaning and a dignity and, what is less, a hope of ultimate blessedness. But again the austerity is chilling. When the Roman satirist Juvenal set out to describe the activity of men, he specified prayer, fear, anger, pleasure, joys and conversations as the main constituent parts: but it is with these staples of our existence that the driven-snow God has so little to do. I took the Falklands Islands Thanksgiving Service as an example of the weaknesses of the red-blooded theologies: but what has a driven-snow theologian to say from the pulpit of St Paul's? Nothing, I think, but the appropriateness of repentance. So much fear, anger, triumph, joy, anguish, folly, blood and heroism are to him poured in vain into the South Atlantic. Historically, the driven-snow God is continuous with the God whom Jesus knew and preached, but so much has been taken away from his supposed activity that it is difficult to see him still as a loving heavenly Father. Fathers on earth are concerned to secure the proximate good of their children, that is their happiness, as well as their ultimate good. A father may sometimes say, 'This will be good for your soul', but the words strike a chilling note.

It is John's clarity of mind which is the undoing of his theology. He has taken away too much. He has made it too plain how little there is left. Moving with ceaseless industry from topic to topic, he has shown an honest modern man what it is still possible for him to believe, what can be saved from the wreck. As a structure of possibility, it draws our admiration; as the ghost of its former self, it lacks appeal. Its basis in experience does not seem to me to carry conviction, and its account of the divine action does not outweigh the improbabilities entailed. In a word, John lacks the first virtue of a theologian, obscurity.

6   The Wider God Debate
John Hick

As will be evident from Chapter 4, I agree with Michael that what he calls a 'red-blooded' – I would call it a simplistic – theology, according to which God diverts Exocet missiles or manipulates the brains of cardinals and cabinet ministers, is completely untenable. It conflicts, as I have already argued, with the profounder and more realistic view that God has created us (through a long evolutionary process) as free and responsible beings in an objective environment which functions in accordance with its own laws. Michael sees this theological development, which has emerged strongly during recent centuries, as a desperate attempt to salvage something from the wreckage of earlier theological constructions. I see it differently: as an example of theological development in response to new knowledge and new understanding. Christian thought is not a fixed, unchanging rock, but a living and growing organism. Its inner life consists in a particular stream of religious experience, which demands the framework of understanding which we call Christian theology. As the church moves through different historical environments, embodying new phases of human knowledge, this framework naturally changes and diversifies, taking different forms. No Christian today believes as a third-century or a thirteenth-century Christian believed; for the prevailing world-views in terms of which doctrines are formed on the basis of Christian experience have undergone immense and far-reaching developments over the centuries. But the Christian movement as a whole is stronger, not weaker, for its continuously reformed self-understanding.

Michael seems to think that Christians must either adhere to a pre-modern theology or abandon their faith. But if Christianity is essentially a historical movement, a stream of religious life, participating in the development of human knowledge and civilization, it is entirely natural that its intellectual self-understanding should develop and take fresh forms in new cultural epochs. I therefore do not at all share Michael's stationary conception of theology. Nor am I at all alarmed by his invocation of the eighteenth-century Deists, with their belief in an absent God. If God is absent, why indeed not cease to believe in him? But it is Michael who has followed that path, not myself. I know that God is not absent. We are at all times in his unseen presence. He is only absent in so far as we fail to be conscious of him. But, in reality, in all the affairs of our lives we are having to do with him and he with us.

The correct picture, then, as I see it, is not that God long ago set the world process in motion and has since left it alone. On the contrary, he is creatively present at every moment of time and every point in space, so that it is in principle possible for human beings to be consciously related to him in any phase or region of human history. As William Temple (a great liberal theologian in his own day) wrote some fifty years ago:

> Either all occurrences are in some degree revelation of God, or else there is no such revelation at all; for the conditions of the possibility of any revelation require that there should be nothing which is not revelation. Only if God is revealed in the rising of the sun in the sky can He be revealed in the rising of a son of man from the dead; only if He is revealed in the history of Syrians and Philistines can He be revealed in the history of Israel; only if He chooses all men for his own can He choose any at all; only if nothing is profane can anything be sacred.[1]

The dependence of the universe on God, and its instrumentality to the divine purpose, does not of course depend upon whether the 'big bang' some ten to fifteen billions of years ago was unique or was one of a series, conceivably an infinite series. For creation is not an event at a certain point in time, but is the creation *ex nihilo* of space-time itself. That the physical universe, as a system producing life and spirit (possibly in innumerable worlds), is divinely created means that it exists by the will and for the purpose of God.

Michael raises again the question of God as the final explanation of the world. As indicated earlier (p. 33), I believe that the existence of an eternal being, the uncreated creator of everything that exists other than himself, provides the only possible final stopping-point for our 'Why?' questions. In face of the space-time system as a whole we can still properly ask *why* it exists. The question makes sense because it has a possible answer – namely that it is produced by an ultimate uncreated creative power. But we cannot meaningfully ask why an unproduced producer exists, for no more ultimate reality is conceivable by reference to which such a being might be explained. Nothing could, in logic, be more ultimate than the eternal self-existent creator of everything other than himself. As I said above (pp. 43f.), however, this is not a proof of God's existence; for it leaves open the possibility that there is in fact *no* answer to the question 'Why does the universe exist?' But to see the unique ultimacy of the concept of God is to see the explanatory power of that concept. This perception opens the door to belief in the reality of God.[2] But, as I have already acknowledged, it cannot by itself propel anyone through that door. The positive impetus comes from religious experience.

Michael finds implausible the thought that the meaning of our human existence lies in the possibility of gradual growth, through our experience of life in this and future environments, into fully human beings, fulfilling at last God's creative purpose for us. It is true that we cannot confirm from present observation that this is so; for in some men and women we see growth in grace and love, whilst in others we see a hardening into selfishness. But any creation of human animals through their own freedom into perfected children of God must take far longer than this present earthly life. Further, it requires that the continuation of life in other environments beyond death is not simply a straight prolongation; nor must it involve (as Michael suggests) a withdrawal of our freedom, but rather relative new beginnings through some kind of *bardo* phase, such as is suggested by the Buddhist tradition and tentatively explored in my book, to which Michael refers, *Death and Eternal Life*.[3] Obviously the later stages of our creation lie beyond our present horizon, and any pictures that we may form of them can be no more than conjectural. But that we are indeed part of a great creative process, which involves a continued life or lives, seems to me to follow from faith in the loving heavenly Father revealed to us through Jesus.

Michael finds no religious appeal in the thought that we exist within the loving purpose of God, and finds it impossible to accept that the profound dimension of pain and suffering is the measure of the cost of creation through creaturely freedom. He does not accept that perfected personal life, with responsible freedom at its core, could justify such a price. We touch here upon vast issues concerning the age-old problem of evil, at which we have only been able to glance in these chapters. I have myself written at length about this challenge to religious faith in *Evil and the God of Love*, and should like to refer the reader to this book.[4] I accept that to those who have no positive ground for religious belief within their own experience the problem of evil can be an insuperable barrier. But what of those of us who are sometimes conscious of existing in the unseen presence of God – a consciousness which can occur in dark moments of suffering and setback and danger as well as in the sunlit moments of success and happiness? To share in this consciousness is to participate in one of the historical forms of a world-wide experience. And I have been arguing in this book that it is entirely reasonable and sane for us to trust this form of experience and to proceed to believe and to live on the basis of it. Michael does not seem to me to have offered any counter to this central argument. Instead he has been describing how things seem to one who does *not* participate in the field of religious experience; and from that vantage point he finds no reason to believe in God. But from the very different vantage point of those who participate, even if only peripherally, in the experience of existing in God's presence, there is the option of trusting that experience as cognitive of reality. We are free either to take the risk of accepting our religious experience, together with that of the tradition of which we are part, as veridical, or to take the contrary risk of rejecting it as illusory. My claim is that it is fully reasonable, rational and sane to accept this experience as authentic, and thus to allow the divine presence increasingly to dawn upon us.

It is not possible to spell out a positive contemporary theology within the narrow limits of the present discussion. I have tried to do this elsewhere, in a book appearing at about the same time as this one.[5] I must invite readers to consider it and to judge for themselves whether a thoroughly modern version of Christianity is a live option for today. Large issues are involved. Indeed, all the topics that we have discussed here open out on to other major issues in the philosophy of religion and theology.

We have not, for example, discussed the various attempted disproofs of God's existence (claiming that the concept of God is incoherent and therefore such that it could not possibly be instantiated); and the various naturalistic interpretations of religion as illusion – of which the most influential are probably the Freudian theory, the sociological hypothesis of Durkheim and others, and the Marxist analysis of religion, building upon Feuerbach's projection theory. Like the theistic arguments, none of these has proved to be generally convincing.[6] Michael has relied on the agreed fact that it is always possible for apparently cognitive experience to be illusory, and has claimed that it is more reasonable to believe that apparently cognitive religious experience is not, than that it is, an effect in human consciousness of the presence of an environing divine reality. We have discussed this issue fairly fully – within the limitations of the space available – and this discussion did not require us to take up the specific naturalistic theories. Indeed, we are agreed that the universe is religiously ambiguous, in the sense that it is in principle possible to offer both complete and consistent naturalistic interpretations and complete and consistent religious interpretations of it. The theologian is then of course under an obligation to suggest why, if God exists, the universe should be religiously ambiguous; and his explanation hinges upon the need to preserve our cognitive freedom in relation to God. The agnostic can, however, remain agnostic about this entire theological package, as indeed Michael does.

A neighbouring issue which we have not been able to take up within the confines of this short book is that of science and religion. The general assumption prevailing within a science and technology-oriented culture such as our own is that every circumstance and event has a purely natural cause. This assumption militates against religious belief by leading people to feel that a non-religious account of religious experience must be preferable to a religious one. On the other hand, the naturalistic assumption has itself been strongly criticized as being no more than a cultural assumption, and a groundless one at that. In polar opposition to this assumption is the belief of some that there are today positive scientific grounds for belief in God, in the form of a new kind of design argument based upon current cosmological and astrophysical theories. However, the whole topic of the bearing of science on religion is one that we could not attempt to pursue here.

Yet another issue which arises at a certain point of the God debate concerns the plurality and variety of concepts of God, and of the corresponding forms of experience of God or of the ultimately Real. There are not only the different, though overlapping, visions of God within the other great theistic traditions – Islam, Judaism, theistic Hinduism, Sikhism, African 'primal' religion. There are also the various ways of conceiving and experiencing the Real as non-personal in advaitic Hinduism and in Buddhism. Is not belief in the divine, or the transcendent, undermined by this very variety? The question is an entirely proper one; and I believe that the correct answer is No. But this is yet another large topic that we could not discuss either in our day-long debate or in this printed version of it.

Looking in yet another direction, we were at times on the verge of large and difficult historical questions concerning the Old and New Testaments. To what extent did the great religious figures of the past, including Jesus, share the world-view of their time, and to what extent did this affect the ways in which they experienced both the world and their own relationship to God? How literally should we understand the miracle stories with which the scriptures abound? And so on. A complete discussion of the God question, as it confronts us within the Judaeo-Christian tradition, would have to go into the whole subject of biblical interpreation.[7]

It is thus evident – and as evident to the authors as to anyone else – that we have only been discussing one aspect of the large and many-sided question of the reasonableness of belief in God. However, if one has to pick out a single aspect as central, religious experience seems to us to be the right one to select today. But a larger treatment would have to include far more. In the meantime, Michael and I agree to differ. I remain a believer in the reality of God, whilst he remains agnostic.

Let me end by relating our discussions here to another branch of the contemporary debate about God, that focussed by Don Cupitt's two recent books, *Taking Leave of God* and *The World to Come*.[8] He also, like Michael, has arrived at a kind of atheism, though in Don's case it is a religious atheism, or religious naturalism, which he describes as a form of Christian Buddhism.

Michael and Don were both contributors to *The Myth of God*

Incarnate,[9] to which I contributed whilst also being the editor. In this book we argued (amongst other theses) that the idea of divine incarnation is a mythic, or metaphorical, rather than a literal idea. To say that Jesus is the Son of God is to use poetic diction expressing, in language which was familiar and natural in the ancient Near East, his lordship in relation to ourselves, as the one through whom we have encountered God's saving activity on earth. It will not have escaped the notice of some more conservative Christians that two of the seven theologians who thus collaborated to identify the myth of God incarnate have now gone on to speak of the myth of God. Must this not be disturbing to the other five of us? Does it not show – our more conservative friends may ask – that once you begin to question the received teaching of the church there is no stopping place short of outright atheism?

I cannot speak for my fellow authors of *The Myth*. For my own part, I do see the Goulder and Cupitt moves as revealing both the difficulties and the dangers of serious and fundamental theological thinking today. It is clearly much safer to sit tight within the tradition and ask no difficult questions! But safety is not necessarily everything. William James pointed out the important psychological distinction between those scholars who are dominated by the desire to seek the truth and those who are dominated by the desire to avoid error. You can avoid the risk of error by renouncing all questioning and experimentation; but you will thereby forfeit the possibility of attaining to larger visions and greater truth. And if, out of a group of seven theological experimenters in the search for greater truth, two have (in the opinion of the other five) fallen into error, this may well reflect the real difficulty of the God question within our contemporary Western culture. Needless to say, these particular seven are only a more or less random selection out of the very many contemporary theologians who have long been experimenting in the same direction. The only distinctiveness of the seven *Myth* authors was that their book happened to come at the right time to break through a psychological log-jam in popular attitudes in Britain to the doctrine of the incarnation. Discussion of the subject, in Britain, has become much freer;[10] and for many a major watershed has been passed in accepting that it is not after all such a terrible thought that divine incarnation is a mythic, or metaphorical, notion.

This fact had been obscured by the aura of sacred mystery

surrounding the idea of the Trinity, which functions as a protective envelope around the notion of divine incarnation. Once we go beyond the popular imagery of three heavenly super-persons, no one professes to understand the doctrine of the Trinity. It is accordingly regarded as a mystery which we must believe although we cannot expect to understand it. What is forgotten is that it is not a divinely revealed truth but a humanly constructed formula. The Christian mind has created a poetic image which does not have any accepted prose translation. Like so many poetic phrases, it can be interpreted in a variety of ways; and indeed its power lies precisely in its untranslatability and rational incomprehensibility. It shares this quality with the idea of divine incarnation, which lives – surely we have all found this to be so – in the poetry of Christmas rather than in the prose of philosophy or theology.

I do not then, as editor of *The Myth*, see it as a tragedy that two of the book's contributors have moved into agnosticism and religious naturalism; but rather as a realistic indication of the difficulties of honest belief in God today among those who are of an open and questioning mind.

I have indicated in Chapter 2 and the beginning of Chapter 4 and the beginning of this chapter where I disagree with Michael. My disagreement with Don is at a different point. He is presenting a religious naturalism which has some affinities with Buddhism and which seems to be making an increasing appeal today[11] – though more outside than inside the churches. My difference from him, and from others who are thinking in similar ways, concerns the relationship between religious ideas and experiences on the one hand, and on the other hand the transcendent divine Reality to which they ostensibly refer. But first let us take note of what Don is saying.

He wants religion to become 'autonomous'. Kant has taught us the idea of the autonomy of ethics. To be rational involves being able to distinguish between morally rational and morally irrational behaviour. And as rational agents we are conscious of an obligation to do the right simply because it is right. Ethics does not depend upon any external authority, whether human or divine, or upon any sanctions, either in this or another world. Its authority is intrinsic to the moral consciousness itself. Thus morality is not a response to a reality beyond us, but consists essentially in the integrity of our own inner nature. And Don argues that religion should have a parallel kind of autonomy. As spiritual beings we are conscious of an inner call to attain to unselfish and therefore universal and impartial love, thus 'becoming spirit' or being spiritualized. Don calls this 'the religious requirement'. And he holds that the religious requirement does not depend upon any external power or authority. It arises from within our own nature as the kind of spiritual beings that we are.

At this point, it seems to me, it is desirable to distinguish between religion more generally and theistic religion in particular. There are very impressive non-theistic forms of religion, of which the Buddhisms (Theravada and Mahayana) are two. Described negatively Buddhism, in both of its main forms, is atheistic. But if a Christian becomes a Buddhist, rather than say, negatively, that he has ceased to believe in the reality of God, it would be far better to describe the situation positively by saying that he has become illuminated by the *Dharma*. He has found the ultimately Real, not as a personal Face, but as the non-personal Dharmakaya, or Nirvana, or Sunyata. Can someone be illuminated by the Dharma, with its profound analysis of the human situation and its compelling ideal of the selfless person, and yet continue to believe in the reality of God as Christianity conceived? Some (for example, John Cobb)[12] have argued with considerable persuasiveness that this *is* possible. But whether it is or not, this does not seem to be what Don is doing. He seems to want to be a non-theistic Christian Buddhist; and of course the inevitable question is whether it might not be better to maintain the distinction between theistic Christianity and non-theistic Buddhism and accept a Buddhist identity.

However, at this point there is, as it seems to me, an ambiguity in Don's programme. One possibility – the less radical one – would be to say, not that there is no God, but that true religion requires us to pursue our own spiritual integrity independently of him. We ought to live autonomously, as if there were no God. To live thus, *etsi deus non daretur*, was characterized by Bonhoeffer as 'religion come of age'; and this is what is suggested by the title *Taking Leave of God*, derived from Eckhart's dictum, 'Man's last and highest parting is when, for God's sake, he takes leave of God.' But despite this intriguing title, it seems clear that in fact Don intends the more radical move of saying that God, conceived as a reality which exists independently of us and who has created us, is an illusion. God is a fictional being, a *focus imaginarius*, formed by the projection of our religious ideas upon the universe. Although there are occasional ambiguous passages, Don generally opts for this more radical alternative. He speaks of 'the objectively atheous position here propounded'.[13] 'God,' he says, 'is not an actually-existing individual person. God is a humanly-needed way of speaking generated by the impact of the religious demand and ideal upon us.'[14] Again, God is 'the unifying symbol that eloquently personifies and represents to us everything that spirituality requires of us'.[15] And, 'the doctrine of God is an encoded set of spiritual directives'.[16] Accordingly, 'God can be demythologized into spirituality without,' he claims, 'religious loss.'[17]

The big question is, of course, whether God can indeed be demythologized, and regarded as an imaginative personification of spirituality, without religious loss. There would be no loss for a Buddhist, for he or she experiences and responds to ultimate reality in a quite different way from the Christian. However, it would not be correct to say that a Buddhist demythologizes the idea of God, the ultimate creator of the universe; for this idea plays no part in Buddhist understanding. But I am going to argue that there would be serious religious loss in 'demythologizing' God within Christianity's inalienably theistic experience of the divine.

However, let me first take note of some of the valid insights with which Don supports his central thesis. These are truths that are obscured by the traditional form of theism against which he is reacting. I want to note them, partly because they are true and important, and partly in order to point out that they do not necessarily commit one to atheism, whether religious or otherwise. That requires, in addition, a leap of atheistic faith. Don is entitled to make that leap; but others of us are equally entitled to make the contrary leap of theistic faith.

First, he is right, surely, in rejecting the pre-modern idea of God as omnipotently determining the course of events constituting the world, and as occasionally issuing special commands and performing special favours in the form of miraculous answers to prayer. The belief that God acts in that way is part of what he calls heteronomous faith. If we believe in the reality of God today, however, we must, as I have argued in Chapter 4, believe that God has created us as genuinely though limitedly free beings, exercising our freedom in an objective environment which functions in accordance with its own laws, so that God does not over-ride either the structure of that environment or our creaturely freedom. And so we can have some sympathy with Don's quizzical comments on those who profess the older conception of the interfering God and yet do not take it seriously in practice:

> I have noticed for some years that many of my Christian friends who profess heteronomous faith feel obliged to make little jokes about it. If misfortune strikes them they say jokingly that God must be annoyed; they joke about thunder and lightning as manifestations of God's displeasure; they joke about praying for rain or for victory in some contest or other; and although they profess in general terms to believe in signs of God's providence and the discernment of God's will, they laugh at the naivety of one who applies these beliefs in a concrete and specific way to just one particular case.[18]

If that is what heteronomous faith is, many of us including Michael will agree that such faith is mistaken. But I maintain that we do not have to jump all the way from the interfering God to atheism. We may believe in a God who respects the freedom that he has given to his human creatures and who preserves the autonomy of the world in which he has placed them.

Second, Don is right, surely, in rejecting any equation of true religion with belief in a body of theological propositions. 'Christianity in particular,' he says, 'seems almost to identify being a religious believer with assenting to a large body of highly implausible assertions about supernatural beings and events.'[19] Regardless of whether this or that theological proposition is plausible, Christian faith does not consist in believing propositions. True religion, in my view, is the response of the whole person to the ultimate Reality which is conceived and experienced in different ways from within the various great world faiths; and doctrines are human attempts to understand the implications of a given strand of religious experience. As such they are inherently fallible and reformable, and should never be accorded an absolute status. But once again, it does not follow from this understanding of doctrine that there is no God; nor, of course, does Don suggest any such entailment. He does, however, proceed through these valid insights to his atheistic conclusion; and it is therefore worth observing that a considerable part of his discussion is more or less standard contemporary liberal theology, and does not by any means amount to or require the religious atheism which he himself espouses.

The third point on which we can agree with Don concerns 'the culturally evolved and symbolic character of religious belief'.[20] He develops this in several interesting historical chapters, tracing the evolution of the Western outlook since the Renaissance. He shows how the mediaeval heteronomous consciousness, which held its beliefs on authority, has grown into the modern autonomous consciousness, which requires us to see truths for ourselves rather than accept them on any external authority. This is a cultural development, and it has carried with it, as Don shows, important consequences for Western religious thinking. But of course autonomous thinking should not be equated by definition with thinking that there is no God; nor does seeing truths for oneself exclude that the reality of God may be a truth that one sees for oneself. The modern revolt against external authorities obviously cannot, in so far as it is rational, be equated with the dogmatic denial of an ultimate reality in which being and value are one.

A fourth important truth is his emphasis on the symbolic, rather than literal, character of much religious language. This brings out the element of truth in the neo-Wittgensteinian view of religious utterance as an autonomous language game, not subject to external criteria or criticism. Religious doctrines are not literal descriptions of the divine Reality. Rather, they are symbols pointing to that Reality by helping us to become conscious of it. And as symbols they have an optional character. For different symbol systems, drawn from different cultural sources, have developed within the various religious traditions. And these systems do each constitute something like a Wittgensteinian 'language game'. They function, to a great extent, as independent and alternative systems. Thus Jews speak of the God of Israel and of his interactions with the Jewish people; and the figure (for example) of Shiva does not appear at all in distinctively Jewish religious discourse. Likewise in the Shaivite tradition of India one speaks of the many-faceted Shiva; and the figure of Yahweh does not appear in this Indian world of religious discourse. And yet at the same time whilst these are two different languages, they are both languages about the same thing, namely the ultimate divine Reality, and are both means by which people seek to articulate their relationship to that reality.

But that religious language is symbolic and that it forms alternative systems, does not entail that it fails to point to any reality beyond the human. The alternative possibility is that the symbols of the different religions point in their different ways to a Reality which transcends them all. And indeed it may, as I shall argue presently, be religiously necessary to affirm the ultimate Reality which exceeds all our human religious symbols but is variously and partially perceived through them all. Don comes very close to saying this when, in one of his more positive passages, he says that 'if you recognize the culturally evolved and symbolic character of religious belief, and see that beyond all the imagery and beyond the limits of language there is only and can only be the deep peace and silence of the Ineffable, you are liberated'.[21] If Don is pointing to the limitless divine Reality which exceeds the reach of all human language, he has re-joined the more mystical side of the religious traditions. He may then be open to the witness of the mystics that the Real can be pointed to not only with such terms as 'silence' and 'peace' but also with such terms as 'life', 'ground', 'creative power'. *Satchitananda* ('Being-consciousness-happiness'), *al Haq* ('the Real').

The fundamental question concerning religious language is whether it *only* expresses certain human states of mind or whether it *also* points, even though always with finite symbols, to an ultimate Reality which is limitlessly more beingful and more valuable than our little human egos. If religious language is *only* expressive, and does not refer to a divine Reality beyond us, then the God of which it ostensibly speaks is a figment of our imaginations. God has no reality independently of human beings, and indeed did not exist before the human imagination created him. God is not then the eternal self-existent creator of the universe, and hence a possible ground of hope for his creatures, but is merely a thought in the consciousness of a recently evolved and perhaps fleeting form of animal life on a small planet of a minor star on the edge of one of the millions of millions of galaxies. If this is the case, we would do well to face its implications squarely, as the greatest humanist thinkers have done. Thus Bertrand Russell wrote in a famous passage to which Don refers:[22]

That Man is the product of causes which had no prevision of the end they were achieving; that his origin, his growth, his hopes and fears, his loves and beliefs, are but the outcome of accidental collocations of atoms; that no fire, no heroism, no intensity of thought and feeling, can preserve an individual life beyond the grave; that all the labours of the ages, all the devotion, all the inspiration, all the noonday brightness of human genius, are destined to extinction in the vast death of the solar system, and that the whole temple of Man's achievement must inevitably be buried beneath the debris of a universe in ruins – all these things, if not quite beyond dispute, are yet so nearly certain, that no philosophy which rejects them can hope to stand. Only within the scaffolding of these truths, only on the firm foundation of unyielding despair, can the soul's habitation henceforth be squarely built.[23]

The difference then between those who believe, with the Christian tradition, that theistic language points beyond itself, and those who, like Don, see it as turned inward in self-reference, is the difference between the presence and the absence of hope for the human spirit. Or rather, it is the difference between there being hope only for a spiritual elite and hope for the whole human race. For there are those comparatively rare individuals who can find peace and fulfilment in pursuing the ideal of selfless love on the understanding both that there is no transcendent divine Reality and that this present earthly life constitutes the entirety of human existence. But they are a small elite. For the great mass of humanity through the ages life has been a harsh struggle for survival, a struggle which has inevitably evoked self-regarding fear, anxiety, envy and jealousy amid threats of imminent pain and starvation. In the words of Barbara Ward and René Dubos at the 1972 Stockholm Conference on the Human Environment:

The actual life of most of mankind has been cramped with back-breaking labour, exposed to deadly or debilitating disease, prey to wars and famines, haunted by the loss of children, filled with fear and the ignorance that breeds more fear. At the end, for everyone, stands dreaded unknown death. To long for joy, support and comfort, to react violently against fear and anguish is quite simply the human condition.[24]

In face of this human situation (as I pointed out in Chapter 2),[25] the message of the great world religions, arising from their distinctive

110

forms of religious experience, has been that there is a limitlessly higher and better Reality in relation to which or in union with which we can be transformed. This transformation, or perfecting, is manifestly only begun, in the large majority of us, in the course of this present life. But the great religions all teach that our total existence transcends our present earthly career, whether by resurrection or by reincarnation. It is because God is real, and because God is gracious and opens to us the richness of his eternal life, that there is a basis of hope, not only for the elite few but for all humanity.

To draw out the contrast between the basic pessimism of atheism, including Don's religious and Michael's secular atheisms, and the basic optimism of the great religions, is not of course to establish the truth of the more hopeful alternative. Whether it is reasonable for us to believe, amid the ambiguities of the world in which we find ourselves, in the reality of God and hence in the ultimate goodness of Reality, is the question that we have been debating in this book. I have argued that if one participates, however slightly, in the field of religious experience, then it is reasonable and sane to take the risk of trusting this form of experience as an authentic, though variously clouded, contact with divine Reality and to proceed to live and to believe on the basis of it.

But Michael, standing outside this field of religious experience, does not trust it and does not accept that anyone else can properly trust it either. And so our debate has ended in disagreement. We can both join, however, in hoping that it has opened up central issues for renewed discussion. There can be no more important question than that of the reality of God, and our joint aim is to help others to focus their thoughts upon this.

Notes

Chapter 1 The *Fram* Abandoned

1. Austin Farrer, *Faith and Speculation*, New York University Press 1967; Brian Hebblethwaite, *Religious Studies* 14, pp. 223–36.
2. John A. T. Robinson, *Honest to God*, SCM Press, London, and Westminster Press, Philadelphia 1963.
3. Don Cupitt, *The World to Come*, SCM Press 1982, pp. xiif.

Chapter 2 Our Experience of God

1. Mahatma Gandhi, *All Men are Brothers*, Columbia University Press, New York 1958, p. 79.
2. William James, *The Varieties of Religious Experience* (1902), Collins Fontana 1981, p. 75.
3. Ibid., p. 81.
4. Timothy Beardsworth, *A Sense of Presence*, The Religious Expereince Unit, Oxford 1977, p. 120.
5. Ibid., p. 122.
6. Alister Hardy, *The Spiritual Nature of Man*, The Clarendon Press, Oxford 1979, p. 53.

Chapter 3 How Dependable is Experience?

1. Wolfhart Pannenberg, *Jesus – God and Man*, SCM Press, London and Westminster Press, Philadelphia, 1968, ch. 3.
2. Trevor Ling, *The Significance of Satan*, SPCK 1961.
3. Timothy Beardsworth, *A Sense of Presence*, p. 9.
4. Ibid., p. 7.
5. Ibid., p. 30.
6. Ibid., pp. 31f.

Chapter 4 Prayer, Providence and Miracle

1. John Hick, *Faith and Knowledge*, Macmillan, London and Cornell University Press, Ithaca[2] 1967; Collins Fontana 1969, ch. 6.

2. See, for example, H. C. Rümke, *The Psychology of Unbelief: Character and Temperament in Relation to Unbelief*, Rockliffe, London 1952.
3. Thomas Aquinas, *Summa contra Gentiles*, Book III, ch. 101.
4. David Hume, *Enquiry*, Section X, Part I.
5. George Meredith, *The Ordeal of Richard Feverel*, ch. 13.

Chapter 5   The Action of God

1. Emil Brunner, *Christianity and Civilization*, 2 vols, James Nisbet, London 1948, 1949.
2. In a lecture given in Birmingham Cathedral, 9 May 1977.
3. See the dialogue on 'The Intelligibility of the Universe' between Hugo Meynell and Harry Stopes-Roe in *Reason and Religion* ed. Stuart Brown, Cornell University Press 1977.

Chapter 6   The Wider God Debate

1. William Temple, *Nature, Man and God*, Macmillan, London and New York 1934, p. 306.
2. For a fuller treatment of this point see my *Arguments for the Existence of God*, Macmillan, London and Herder and Herder, New York 1970.
3. John Hick, *Death and Eternal Life*, Collins, London and Harper and Row, New York 1976; Collins Fontana 1979.
4. John Hick, *Evil and the God of Love*, Macmillan and Collins Fontana, London 1966 and Harper and Row, New York 1967.
5. John Hick, *The Second Christianity*, SCM Press, London 1983.
6. I have discussed this problem in *God and the Universe of Faiths*, Macmillan, London and St Martin's Press, New York 1973, Collins Fount 1974; and in *God has Many Names*, Macmillan, London 1980 and Westminster Press, Philadelphia 1982.
7. Michael has written about some of these questions in 'Jesus, the Universal Man of Destiny', ch. 3 of *The Myth of God Incarnate* ed. John Hick, SCM Press, London and Westminster Press, Philadelphia 1977.
8. *Taking Leave of God*, SCM Press, London and Crossroad Publishing Company, New York 1980; *The World to Come*, SCM Press, London 1982.
9. *The Myth of God Incarnate* ed. John Hick, SCM Press, London and Westminster Press, Philadelphia 1977.
10. See, for example, *God Incarnate: Story and Belief* ed. Anthony E. Harvey, SPCK 1981.
11. See, for example, George Rupp, *Beyond Existentialism and Zen*, OUP, New York 1979; Gordon D. Kaufman, *The Theological Imagination*, Westminster Press, Philadelphia 1981.

12. John B. Cobb, *Beyond Dialogue*, Westminster Press, Philadelphia 1982.
13. Don Cupitt, *Taking Leave of God*, p. 13.
14. Ibid., p. 133.
15. Ibid., p. 9.
16. Ibid., p. 101.
17. Don Cupitt, *The World to Come*, p. xiv.
18. *Taking Leave of God*, p. xi.
19. Ibid., p. xii.
20. *The World to Come*, p. xvii.
21. Ibid., p. xvii.
22. Ibid., p. vii.
23. Bertrand Russell, *Mysticism and Logic and Other Essays*, Edward Arnold, London 1918, pp. 47f. In 1962 Russell wrote in a letter: 'My own outlook on the cosmos and on human life is substantially unchanged' (*Autobiography*, Vol. III, Allen and Unwin, London and Simon and Schuster, New York 1969, p. 173).
24. Barbara Ward and René Dubos, *Only One Earth*, Penguin Books, Harmondsworth and Norton, New York 1972, p. 35.
25. See above, p. 32.

Index